KEEPING AN OPEN DOOR

KEEPING AN OPEN DOOR

Passages in a University Presidency

Keith Brodie and Leslie Banner

Duke University Press *Durham and London 1996*

Printed in the United States of America on acid-free paper ∞
Typeset in Janson Text by Tseng Information Systems, Inc.
Library of Congress Cataloging-in-Publication Data
appear on the last printed page of this book.

For Brenda and Dick

Contents

Preface

This volume is the partial record of an era in American higher education as viewed from the office of one university president. It is not meant to be a complete accounting, but rather a series of observations about the circumstances and the issues that occupied not only those of us concerned with the workings of Duke University but also those like us at research universities across the nation. If there is an overarching theme to be found here, it is that of the responsibilities of citizenship—of students, faculty, and trustees to one another; of the university to American society and the form of government under which we flourish; of all of us in the academic community to the world at large, where human and ecological catastrophes have kept pace with our best efforts to investigate, analyze, synthesize, mediate, inspire, create, solve, and heal with our tools of research and education.

The introductory essay and speeches that follow are windows on the years 1982–1993, when I served as chancellor and then president of Duke. With one exception,[1] we have resisted the urge to substitute a more felicitous phrase, update data, or generalize specific references—in short, to edit the speeches. We think of them as responses to the contemporary moment, and as such, any lasting value lies in their usefulness as primary material.

1. See the introduction to "What It Means to Be a Duke Athlete."

The introductions to the speeches provide historical context, and "Some Notes on a University Presidency" is not intended to be all inclusive but rather complementary—a way to tell a bit more of the story.

Acknowledgments

While this volume is grounded primarily in the Brodie chancellor and presidential files, we are most grateful for the numerous friends and colleagues at Duke who generously took the time to check their own memories and files for us as these pages were being prepared. Of those we consulted, the most often interrupted was Duke University Archivist Dr. William E. King, who once again proved himself an irreplaceable resource. We offer special thanks to him and to his unfailingly conscientious staff in the Duke University Archives, Tom Harkins and Dan Daily. For the photographs in this volume we are indebted to Les Todd, who not only took many of the photos we chose but who also diligently searched the files in the office of the university photographer to find them for us.

In the Office of the President at Duke University, Kay L. Bowman provided invaluable research and office support during the hectic but rewarding days when these speeches were originally written, and we continue to be grateful. In the Office of the President Emeritus (Brodie), we owe much to the unflappable patience of staff assistant Heidi D. Hannah, who performed numerous essential services as this project got underway, including introducing us to the wonders of the internet. We are now thoroughly dependent on her successor, Steven A. Kelts, research assistant and office troubleshooter par excellence.

1

SOME NOTES ON A UNIVERSITY PRESIDENCY

The role of chancellor as deputy president was peculiar to the Sanford era at Duke University where the title "chancellor" had previously been used only twice before: in 1949 as an honorific for President Robert Lee Flowers when he stepped down for the new president, Hollis Edens; and in March of 1969, when Barnes Woodhall was named chancellor pro tem to head a committee of three officers who administered the university until Terry Sanford's arrival in April of 1970. In fact, Duke was unusual among universities in having both a president and a chancellor rather than one or the other to head the institution, but this arrangement reflected the need for a strong manager within the Sanford inner circle. Having a second-in-command allowed Terry, a former governor of North Carolina, to carry out the cultivation of donors, address a large number of alumni associations across the country, and seek the office of president of the United States twice from the Allen Building, Duke's administrative center. He was also able to serve on several corporate boards of directors, all of which created a hectic travel schedule. Yet he was always present when needed and was a constant source of wisdom, energy, and enthusiasm for the many campus projects which he initiated.

When Terry asked me to become his third chancellor beginning in July of 1982, following John Blackburn and A. Kenneth Pye (who later became president of Southern Methodist University), I was taken by surprise. I knew and respected Ken, who had chaired the university's Long-Range Planning Committee during my period of service on it (1977–81), and it was an honor to be asked to succeed him. But I had little understanding of what the position entailed and had given it no thought, for at the time I was firmly oriented toward the Medical Center. The Department of Psychiatry, which I had come from Stanford to chair, was developing well, and I had plans for my coming year (1982–83) as president of the American Psychiatric Association. Thus, while I was aware that the chancellor search committee had met privately and given Terry a short list, it came as a shock when he called me during dinner one Saturday night and asked if I would meet with him to discuss the position. Although my service on the Executive Committee of the Academic Council (1976–78) had previously brought us together, the president of Duke remained an enigma to me. Undeniably, Terry Sanford was exciting to be around, and under his leadership Duke was doing well. The idea of working for him was intriguing, and so I agreed, not knowing exactly what was involved.

What was involved proved to be the nuts-and-bolts administering of the place under Terry's watchful eye. Essentially, I served as his alter ego, coordinating and integrating administrative and auxiliary services and collaborating with the provost in shaping and supporting the academic mission of the university. When Bill Bevan left the provostship in the fall of 1982, Terry also asked me to assume the role of acting provost. This I did, working more closely with him than ever and learning more than I could have imagined.

Terry had agreed that as chancellor I could continue to teach and see patients weekly. After a three-year term I would continue in my academic appointment as James B. Duke Professor of Psychiatry in the Medical Center. Maintaining a base there was important to me for I saw the university chancellorship as an opportunity to learn more about higher education, not as preparation for the presidency. Such a progression was not in my mind, nor had it been mentioned to me when I accepted the job. When the search went forward for Terry's successor, I told several members of the search committee that I did not want to be considered. Later, after the search had been on for some time without yielding a strong consensus candidate, the committee asked me to meet with them and answer questions about the "ideal president" from my perspective as chancellor. Following that meeting, Neil Williams, chair of Duke's Board of Trustees, asked me to reconsider being a candidate. I was surprised and at first not inclined to change my mind. But my wife, Brenda, pointed out that this would be the only sure way to see to fruition the initiatives I had undertaken as chancellor. That was enticing, and I agreed.

The professional path I followed to the Duke presidency may seem logical and therefore not unusual, but it is in fact rare to see all these promotions and experiences—departmental chair, faculty governance representative, chancellor, acting provost, president—occurring at the same institution. This single-institution career trajectory had advantages and disadvantages. From the trustees' point of view one clear advantage was that, having liked and approved of the course Terry had charted for Duke, they believed they could assure that the momentum established under his leadership would be maintained by electing his chief operating officer as his successor. The trustees knew that I felt comfortable with hands-on management of the institution and could, therefore, save Duke money—well over a million dollars in the course of my presidency as it turned out—by eliminating the need for a chief operating officer's salary, office expenses, and staff. They also knew that Terry had involved me in a number of key searches—for a provost, a minister to the university, a vice president for development and alumni affairs, the dean of the School of Engineering, the dean of the School of Forestry and Environmental Studies, and the dean of the Divinity School. Thus, when I was named to the presidency, these officers and deans, although newly appointed, felt secure in the knowledge that I had supported their appointments. They could continue as members of my team without the insecurity of having been recently recruited by a departing president.

The trustees were impressed as well with the need for the president to understand the Medical Center. The complex relationship between a medical school, with its hospital and outpatient clinics, and the rest of a university presents an area of constant tension for chief executives of research universities. Because I had chaired a clinical department and served as chief of the psychiatry service for Duke Hospital, as president I could deal from a position of strength with the difficulties of uniting the medical and nonmedical components of the university. I knew that Medical Center administrators had an understandable desire for autonomy based on the very different nature of their enterprise—a desire expressed in the Freudian slip of an ad they sometimes ran for "Duke University Medical Center and Duke University," as if they were two separate institutions. Part of my job both as chancellor and as president was to arbitrate, practically on a daily basis, between the provost and the chancellor for health affairs over academic appointments, shared space, indirect overhead, and donor clearance. Throughout my presidency I looked for ways to ameliorate this tendency of many of the medical staff to work without a sense of oneness with the institution. I well knew that their world of laboratories, around-the-clock shifts, and urgent bedside decision making seemed far removed from the more deliberate pace of scholarship in the arts and sciences. Yet I knew also that most of my medical colleagues joined me in believing that Duke gains immeasurable strength on both sides of the "gauze curtain" from having a medical school that opens its doors onto the tree-shaded lawns of a liberal arts campus and faculty colleagues in other disciplines whose research and teaching can inform and expand their own.

My medical background presented some disadvantage as well,

of course, for I was at times viewed with suspicion by both camps. Despite all I could say and do, faculty outside the Medical Center feared that I would provide only token oversight of the physician-biomedical sciences coalition, allowing Duke's growth to emulate the Johns Hopkins model, where the arts, humanities, and social sciences play a subordinate role to medicine and medical research, and graduate studies receive a greater emphasis than undergraduate education. Duke history lent credence to their concerns, for our medical school had been founded with a core of Hopkins-trained physicians whose influence was still felt. Most of these fears were allayed, I believe, as time passed. My Medical Center colleagues, meanwhile, sometimes wished they did not have to report to a university president who knew their business so well, especially when I temporarily adjusted the financial arrangements to bring a few million dollars from the Medical Center to the core of the university to meet what I, at least, regarded as shared infrastructure needs and responsibilities.

A disadvantage of having already served the university for three years as chancellor was that I had no experience of differing administrative models and fresh approaches to the challenges facing higher education and a Duke University that, thanks to Terry Sanford, was entering an era of newly achieved national stature. With the need in mind to both rejuvenate and inform myself, I had wanted to take a leave of absence during the six months prior to assuming the presidency in July of 1985. But because Terry wanted me on the scene to maintain continuity, I took only enough time to meet with foundation heads and other university presidents. Despite their brevity, these meetings brought me extraordinarily good advice and I returned filled with admiration, optimism, and a renewed enthusiasm for the job. I was especially struck by the way Michael Sovern at Columbia University ran his office and his day. Because several foundation presidents had advised me that he was the most organized president in higher education, I spent half a day watching him in action.

His use of time, his attention to important details while astutely delegating as much as possible to staff, and his enthusiasm for the work he performed were impressive. Later, after assuming the presidency, I spent time with Harold Shapiro (Princeton), Donald Kennedy (Stanford), Bill Friday (the University of North Carolina system), and Jim Freedman (Dartmouth), who provided strong counsel concerning such issues as recruitment of minority faculty, coping with student unrest, surviving the intensity of a presidential schedule, and dealing with trustees.

Despite my three-year apprenticeship with Terry Sanford, I found I had much to learn. Institutional operations had been my proving ground as chancellor, and a year as acting provost had initiated me into the mysteries of administering the arts and sciences and the law, divinity, engineering, forestry, and business schools. But certain other areas had been almost exclusively Terry's purview, including fundraising and speechmaking, athletics, and relations with the trustees. I discovered, in fact, that one of the principal functions of the president is to serve as the intermediary between thirty-six trustees and the university officers and deans. Duke had been blessed with some outstanding trustees over the years—men and women with vision and the capacity to provide support when it was needed. However, I always knew I could count on a handful of trustees to be strong advocates for their own special interests in the university—for the expansion of the Medical Center, for example, or the upgrading of East Campus. In most cases this personal advocacy was completely understandable, even predictable, for unlike corporate boards, whose directors come primarily from outside the corporation and therefore have no reason to identify with any one particular area or division of a company, our trustees are almost entirely alumni and a few parents and grateful patients. Consequently, some on the board are inevitably influenced by their children who are currently Duke students, and many more by their own fond memories of the

Duke they had attended some twenty, thirty, or even forty years before. Thus, former athletes become excited advocates for the athletics department; graduates of our School of Engineering enjoy substantive conversations with Dean Earl Dowell; extracurricular memories of Hoof 'n' Horn (a student theater group) lead to trustee interest in the direction our Drama Program takes; and so on. Furthermore, these tendencies are, if anything, intensified by the frequency with which trustee service overlaps with membership on the boards of visitors that advise and support individual schools and programs throughout the university.

But identifying with components of the university rather than with the whole—although a natural outgrowth of altruistic enthusiasm—frequently leads trustees to neglect their larger corporate responsibilities, especially when partisanship is encouraged from within the institution. The courtship of our trustees by Duke deans and vice presidents sometimes resulted in the development of a contentious and deleterious factionalism within the board. At several of our meetings I began to wonder whether some of the deans had been supplying board members with a too strong dose of their own skepticism with respect to particular policies under discussion, or had encouraged among certain trustees a strong advocacy for the expansion or increased support of the unit they served without regard to the good of the institution as a whole. For example, in the summer of 1991 the board chair and I had concurred in the hope that Duke's next undergraduate tuition increase would be held to 5 percent in light of the increasing public furor over price increases at elite private universities. Yet by December when the full board was ready to discuss the issue, it was reported to me that the dean of the Faculty of Arts and Sciences had begun vigorously lobbying key trustees for more money to increase salaries among his faculty, recruit additional faculty, and hire more support staff. Ultimately, the board went against the president's recommendation and the following May increased tuition by 6.8 percent. I felt that such an increase was unnecessary, and this turned out to be the case as a surplus to budget in excess of $1 million was generated by it.

In most universities such meddling on the part of a dean would be cause for firing; to tolerate it from time to time, a president must be very confident of strong board support. For most of my term there were few battles over policy as public as the tuition contretemps, though keeping our trustees focused on the higher plane of policy setting was often difficult when their personal ties to the university inclined them to become involved in an inappropriate level of detail, including personnel decisions. During the search for a new chancellor of the Medical Center, one influential trustee became so enmeshed in Medical Center politics that he pressured the board to dismiss the search committee, although it comprised key faculty as well as trustees, and simply name his favored internal candidate to the job. Fortunately, the board listened to the president and did not derail the national search process.

My usual strategy in working with the board was political—to work closely with the chair and a small group of leadership trustees, the Executive Committee. I kept them informed about happenings on campus, shared data as it became available, spent time on the telephone and met individually with them, as well as having the provost and my executive vice president for administration meet frequently with selected trustees. Early on, when I realized that the full board also needed to spend more time with me privately, we began to include closed sessions during the quarterly weekend board meetings. Even though there was no audience of reporters or faculty or students for these sessions, these were nonetheless times when I felt considerable pressure because I never knew which issues the trustees might raise. The trustees, however, did not like to be surprised themselves. There is an inherent conflict between rational planning and priority setting, on the one hand, and on the other, moving swiftly to take advantage of opportunities that spontaneously occur. Trustees love plans. They will debate the elements but usually go along with the president's initiatives, especially if those initiatives are launched early enough in the presidency. But rare is the university that does not occasionally find itself face-to-face with an unsolicited opportunity that requires board approval and falls well outside the parameters of the "strategic plan." In these circumstances a board can easily rebel against a well-meaning president, and the institution may lose an influential professor, an important program, or even a building for want of flexibility on the part of the board. Happily, Duke's trustees met that challenge more than once; Duke would never have had the new Terry Sanford Institute building, the Levine Science Research Center, the free-electron laser program and building, or the Washington Duke Inn had it not been for a willingness on their part to accept the president's recommendation to proceed with a project that was not part of the long-range plan for Duke.

One of the most rewarding aspects of my career change from running a medical school department to central university administration lay in the opportunity for closer involvement with our undergraduate colleges and their students. Trinity College had been the original core of Duke University, and the graduates of modern-day Trinity (incorporating the former Woman's College) and the School of Engineering tend to be not only our most numerous but also our most intensely committed alumni. These colleges nurture an age group—the eighteen-to-twenty-two-year-olds—who come to us at an impressionable, idealistic, and energetic time of life. Their enthusiasm is infectious, and the opportunity to make a difference in their lives has rescued for me many a day otherwise bogged down in institutional management. To ensure the quality of the undergraduate student body, Duke had to be—and had to be perceived as being—available to anyone regardless of background, race, or ability to pay. We had noted with concern that, whereas our tuition was less than that charged by Harvard, Yale, Stanford, and Princeton, all these schools had endowments many times greater than our own. It is a marvel that President Sanford and Chancellor John Blackburn had been able to keep our tuition as low as they had during the 1960s and 1970s. In the 1980s, in order to expand our faculty (we moved the student-faculty ratio from 13:1 to 11:1 in Trinity College) and to increase financial aid, we embarked on a two-tiered tuition plan suggested by trustee John Koskinen. This formula fixed tuition increases at roughly the consumer price index plus two percentage points for returning students and charged students entering in 1988 and thereafter a thousand dollars more than returning students. In this way we generated new revenues of approximately $2 million a year for a four-year period and were able to increase our financial aid budget substantially. Thus, funds for financial aid increased during my presidency from $13 million to $30 million annually, and the percentage of the undergraduate student body on need-based aid increased from only 20 percent in 1985 to over 40 percent in 1993.

While addressing the realities of Duke's accessibility, I was also working to change perceptions in order to increase the enrollment of African Americans and North Carolinians. Although Duke is located in a state that is approximately 22 percent black, when I assumed the presidency only 4 percent of our entering class in the undergraduate colleges was comprised of African Americans. It was my view that we needed to increase that number substantially. Few colleges and universities provide the quality of education and the opportunities that are available to Duke undergraduates; and once having graduated from Duke, our alumni do well in gaining admission to the graduate and professional schools of their choice or in pursuing employment—thanks in part to an alumni network interested in hiring Duke graduates. Given these advantages, many of us felt it important to open the doors of the university to all who could benefit. Yet for African American students, Duke seemed to be a remote college option: few applied, and of the few who did, many whom we accepted went elsewhere. Consequently, we embarked on an aggressive recruitment effort to matriculate a critical mass of talented black students such that, by the time I left the presidency in 1993, over 9 percent of our entering class was comprised of African Americans.

The number of North Carolina students at Duke was also low, surprisingly so—less than 10 percent of our entering class. There was a perception in the state that Duke was unaffordable and almost impossible to get into. In 1984 only 272 North Carolina students had their Advanced Placement scores sent to our admissions office, a poor showing compared to the 783 AP scores they had sent to North Carolina State University and the 1,376 that went to the University of North Carolina at Chapel Hill. To counter this problem, we conducted an aggressive campaign of educating counselors in the high schools of our state, and we sought funds from the Duke Endowment, which ultimately provided us with a wonderful grant of $7 million which we were required to match with $3 million from other sources. This $10 million endowment generated funds to allow any student from North or South Carolina who qualified for need-based aid to graduate from Duke without incurring any debt.[1] In other words, all financial aid to these students was on a grant basis; no loans were required. As a result, high school students across the state took notice. By 1993 the number of AP scores submitted to Duke from North Carolina students had increased to 502, and Duke admitted an entering class that year of whom 14 percent were from North Carolina.

1. Although best remembered today for the small family business that became the American Tobacco Company, the Dukes also prospered from the development of water power in North and South Carolina. Thus, in accord with the Duke Indenture, the Duke Endowment provides philanthropic support to institutions and individuals in both of the Carolinas.

To ensure that the administrator in me did not lose touch with the student-faculty point of view, I determined that it was important for Duke's president to teach. I had first taught undergraduate courses at Duke as chair of the psychiatry department in 1979, resuming a practice I enjoyed at Stanford, where I taught human biology to undergraduates. As president I continued my senior seminar in psychology, adding a freshman seminar in psychobiology when we initiated the Freshman Seminar Program. The trustees, however, at my midterm review, asked me to cut back on teaching to free up more time for travel on behalf of the institution. Therefore, during my last four years as president I taught only the freshman seminar, a choice I made because it allowed me to get to know fifteen to twenty students rather well each year and follow their development through subsequent semesters at Duke. About four years into my presidency, at the request of the Student Union Faculty-Student Interaction Committee, I began having lunches on a sign-up basis with students. I also visited fraternities and some of the women's dorms where general discussions usually revolved around career choices as well as what was happening at Duke. Many students turned out for these open-ended discussions which I kept informal and relaxed (one student wrote after such a meeting to "commend" me for not wearing a suit). In January and February each year I would go in the evenings to the first-year dorms to hear how the younger students were doing and to get any complaints they may have had about the admissions process, orientation, or their first semester. It was during those evenings that we learned how bad the teaching of freshman calculus was. I would come back to the Allen Building fuming, "We have got to change this!" and encourage Provost Phillip Griffiths, our James B. Duke Professor of Mathematics, to enter the fray. Together we built up the math department to meet the needs of all of our students, but especially the freshmen. Thanks to Phillip's reputation as a brilliant scholar in the field, we were able to recruit excellent mathematicians from Stanford,

Rice, and Princeton to teach undergraduates as well as contribute to all facets of scholarship.

While college students during my tenure as president were not so radical as they had been in the '60s and '70s, students just down the road at the University of North Carolina at Chapel Hill took over Chancellor Paul Hardin's office (1992), and at Princeton, my alma mater, students twice occupied President Shapiro's office (in 1989 and 1990). I am relieved and happy to say that Duke students did not take over the Allen Building again as they had in 1969, though not for any lack of involvement with issues of social justice both on and off campus. From time to time there was quite a bit of commotion outside my office, students banging on gongs, using p.a. systems on the quad, and rallying for and against a number of issues including divestment (for), low-income housing (for), day care (for), and outside management of our housekeeping staff (against). But as I had faithfully kept open office hours for the students from the very beginning of my presidency, they seemed satisfied to continue scheduling their protests with me, however intensely felt. The most important thing to come out of my regular interactions with students—at the lunches, in the dorms, during office hours, through the seminars I taught, rooting at basketball games, or just walking around campus—was establishing my availability. Students want and need access to the person in charge. While it is difficult for a university president to make the time, it is nevertheless important to do so, to cut through the distance, so that students always know they can come to the president and complain—and many legitimate complaints came to me that way—or to ask for help with personal problems or for support with a project or for academic guidance. Institutions create their own bureaucracies, and time is on the side of the institution. Students come to college excited and eager for their education, wanting to get involved in campus activities, to start something new perhaps, and they have basically three and a half months before the semester ends. A month later they have another three and a half months before the year ends, and then they wait four months to start up again. This cycle is repeated three more times and they graduate. Someone in the administration needs to encourage their ideas and suggestions, remember the things they wanted to change and the things they tried, and carry on with those that prove worthy. Colleges and universities have much to learn from their students; I took the time to listen, and Duke is the better for it.

Well aware of the rising tide of public concern about scandals in college athletics, I turned my attention soon after becoming president to thinking about our athletic programs. We were not having problems at Duke, but I firmly believed then—and almost six years later was borne out by the conclusions of the Knight Commission[2]—that any president of an NCAA institution must take into account the potential for abuse in Division I athletics and take steps to preclude it. To this end I promoted our director of athletics, Tom Butters, to a vice presidency, a position which reported directly to me. As he was in charge of negotiating the many political aspects of our membership in the Atlantic Coast Conference and the National Collegiate Athletic Association and had responsibility for the approximately five hundred students on our athletic teams plus every student at Duke who participated in club or intramural sports, I wanted his advice at the table when officers came together. To his continuing responsibilities

2. The commission, created in 1989 by the trustees of the Knight Foundation to propose reforms for intercollegiate athletics, and co-chaired by William C. Friday and Theodore M. Hesburgh, issued the first of three reports in 1991, stating that it was the commission's "bedrock conviction" that "university presidents are the key to successful reform. They must be in charge—and be *understood* to be in charge—on campuses, in conferences and in the decision-making councils of the NCAA" [Knight Foundation Commission on Intercollegiate Athletics, *Keeping Faith with the Student-Athlete: A New Model for Intercollegiate Athletics*, (March 1991), p. vii].

as director of athletics, I added oversight of our Health, Physical Education, and Recreation Department, thus increasing further his involvement with the education and well-being of our student body. There is a tendency among many educators to assume that people in athletics know only athletics, an assumption as fallacious as assuming that other members of the faculty know only their own areas of scholarly interest and therefore need not be consulted about university administrative matters outside strictly academic bounds. Despite some faculty criticism that the title "vice president" would unnecessarily emphasize or elevate athletics, Duke clearly benefited from having Tom Butters join with the other senior officers in working on broad issues of policy, and it proved to be good and useful for him and for other members of the athletics department to come to a greater awareness of some of the problems the institution was facing and where athletics fit into the overall mission of the university. I am not aware of any other universities that have a director of athletics who is also a vice president; the combination has worked well for us at Duke, probably because the trustees and I had full confidence that Tom Butters would maintain the integrity of our athletics program. As I look back on our success in Division I athletics, I believe it came about because the trustees, the president, the faculty, the director of athletics, the coaches, the support staff, and the students were all proud of Duke's commitment to both academic honesty and winning. If there was a university in the country which stood out as being good at both, it was Duke.

Tom Butters turned out to be as good a judge of character as of athletic talent. His recruitment of Mike Krzyzewski and his loyalty to Mike during the uncertain early years when a new Duke basketball program was being developed proved to be the right thing to do. "Coach K" became the most valuable Duke ambassador on the university's roster of stars. Clearly a brilliant coach and an extraordinary motivator, he has grown into a complete university citizen, speaking in our business school and before alumni groups with the same inspiration and effectiveness he brings to the students in Cameron Indoor Stadium. His remarkable success with basketball has buoyed Duke in many ways, producing an increase in student applications, in attendance at alumni events, in alumni gifts, and in media attention. His teams' four NCAA Final Four appearances followed by back-to-back national championships brought in a financial windfall as well from revenue associated with trademarks, T-shirt sales, logos, gate receipts, and principally, of course, from television. Because I wanted to create a situation whereby people were empowered by their own success, Jack Adcock (the university controller), Tom Butters, and I together developed an incentive agreement: the first half-million dollars of athletics-generated income beyond what we anticipated, i.e., surplus to budget, would always remain in the athletics department. All monies over this $500,000 threshold would go to the university for programs and projects that benefited primarily the undergraduate student body in recognition of their role as the most dedicated and creative fans in the ACC—"the sixth man" on the Duke basketball team. Because the NCAA distributed funds to the universities and their conferences in accordance with each institution's success in the NCAA basketball tournament, for several years the outcome of a single game could make a difference of several hundred thousand dollars to the university, although this was rarely mentioned. In 1990 the NCAA changed its policies regarding the distribution of tournament receipts. All NCAA member institutions were allocated a share based on the number of intercollegiate athletic programs sponsored and the number of athletic scholarships awarded. In addition, approximately one-half of receipts were distributed based on the number of games a school actually played in the tournament over the previous five years. In the Atlantic Coast Conference, member institutions decided to pool receipts from tournament participation and share them equally. No longer did Christian Laettner's single shot in Philadelphia mean a quarter of a million dollars for Duke!

This windfall money allowed the athletics department to fund women's soccer and build the soccer stadium we now have, to refurbish Cameron Indoor Stadium, to provide a new building for our football program and a new baseball diamond in Coombs Field, and to build a jogging trail around our golf course. All these projects were completed with basketball revenues plus gifts to the Athletics Department. Of those basketball revenues that came to the general fund of the university I used a portion to build two lighted astro-turf intramural fields which provided students greater recreational opportunities including extended hours. I used the rest to strengthen the academic programs of the university—principally by enhancing our computing capacity; upgrading classrooms and faculty office space; providing additional support to students through financial aid and special programming; increasing our library holdings; and supporting the library's links with the Triangle Research Libraries Network (TRLN), a consortium formed by Duke, the University of North Carolina at Chapel Hill, and North Carolina State University to create the second largest university library in the nation. In light of this financial success in athletics (unusual among private research universities), it is interesting to note that at one point several members of our faculty concluded that the funding of athletic scholarships should come only from athletic revenues. This might have saved a few thousand dollars for academic initiatives in losing seasons, but the agreement I had forged with Tom Butters brought instead millions of dollars for the support of academic needs.

Excellent new leaders are difficult to find and difficult to appoint. In 1983 the search committee for a new provost to succeed Bill Bevan (and relieve me of the duties of acting provost) had brought in a shortlist of good candidates, all of whom were experienced administrators. But Terry Sanford and I believed Duke was ready for academic leadership unfettered by excessive bureaucratic experience, and so we were prepared to take the risk of seeking as provost a prominent scholar with a vision for Duke's future and little or no administrative background. The right candidate was brought to our attention through one of those serendipitous moments that always seem to attend the discovery of the right person at the right time. A faculty colleague, Morris Weisfeld of the Duke Department of Mathematics, mentioned to Terry a friend, born and reared in North Carolina, a graduate of Wake Forest and Princeton, the Dwight Parker Robinson Professor of Mathematics at Harvard, who, while in Raleigh to attend his father's funeral, had spoken of his desire to return to North Carolina. Several phone calls later Terry and I were on our way to the Duke Faculty Commons to meet this possible candidate, whose academic credentials were indeed impressive and whose administrative experience was near zero. When we entered the commons we noticed a very young man sitting by the window gazing out over the quad. We turned to each other. "Too young," we said. "Can't be our man." We went to the opposite end of the lounge where we sat until the boyish-looking young man approached us. Terry and I looked at each other again. This couldn't be . . . ? He didn't look old enough to be a chaired professor, much less provost material. Fortunately, Phillip A. Griffiths was both (and, in fact, a year older than me). He gave up his chair at Harvard (reputedly the only mathematician ever to do such a thing in the history of the institution) and joined us as James B. Duke Professor of Mathematics and provost from 1984 to 1991.

Phillip Griffiths succeeded in doing what we had hoped for: he strengthened Duke University as an academically challenging center in the arts and sciences, presiding over the birth of innovative programs such as the School of the Environment and the Institute of Statistics and Decision Sciences, internationalizing our programs, and hiring faculty of recognized stature who would serve as magnets to attract other important scholars and the competitive graduate students they expected to train. He and

I both took a lot of heat for this. For example, a review of our English department convinced him that we had a wonderful opportunity to develop a leading department if we appointed as chair an established scholar from outside the university with the vision and the courage to effect change. So it was that we brought Stanley Fish to Duke to occupy an endowed chair in English. He assumed the chairmanship a year after his arrival and brought more visibility and mail to Duke than any one person except basketball coach Mike Krzyzewski. Although initially resisted by many in the department, Stanley brought intellectual excitement, energizing professors who had shown every indication of slowly declining in productivity to retirement. He recruited a group of distinguished senior faculty and extraordinarily promising junior faculty. He brought the department together around the scholarly issues of the day, and when he stepped down from the chairmanship, ultimately to accept appointment as director of Duke University Press, Stanley Fish left to his successor a nationally renowned and respected English department which even his harshest critics acknowledged was the better for his efforts.

When I look back on the phone calls in the night from faculty opposing Stanley's appointment and the hate mail from alumni who claimed falsely that we were abandoning the teaching of the classic literature of Western civilization, I realize how easy it is for institutions to take few risks and accomplish nothing in so doing. There was a time when it would have been far more comfortable to draw back from the development of the massive project that became the Levine Science Research Center. At 335,000 gross square feet, with a construction cost of $46 million, this was the single largest building project outside the Medical Center ever undertaken by the university, and the task of persuading trustees and faculty to endorse the project was daunting. The issues around which debate swirled for nearly three years were financing—obviously a concern because of the large debt to be incurred—and equity. Science faculty in Trinity College and the School of Engineering had become seriously demoralized by a perceived lack of administrative support for their space and research needs. Tensions over space were exacerbated as these faculty saw that their counterparts in the Medical School had far better accommodations, were usually paid on an eleven-month basis (as opposed to nine months for the arts and sciences), and had huge support programs including such amenities as chemical supply centers, centralized systems for water purification, and well ventilated laboratory space that could accommodate modern research needs.

We desperately needed a new science building. Many of our biological science faculty were cramped in substandard space with inadequate ventilation and a tremendous amount of clutter. Science was being conducted in the corridors, with research going on as people walked past. Our computer science department, in which we had made a tremendous investment, continued to be housed in inadequate facilities remote from the other science departments. I am certain these conditions were discouraging many of our students from considering a career in science, as evidenced by the dramatic downturn in the number of students electing most science majors at Duke throughout the 1980s. Not surprisingly, individual science departments initially preferred a separatist approach to solving the facilities problem, proposing that new wings be added to their own existing buildings, and a number of faculty had serious concerns about funding the Levine Center, fearing the effects of having to generate grants and contracts that would produce overhead sufficient to pay the debt service on a large, ambitious, state-of-the-art research building. But Provost Griffiths, Dr. Charles Putman (James B. Duke Professor of Radiology), and I were convinced that interdisciplinary research was the future for Duke and for most research universities and that we could work out a funding scheme that would not jeopardize the university nearly so much as the decline in our capacity to support cutting-edge science was threatening to do.

Charles Putman led the fight for a science center with dedication and persistence. First as vice president for research administration and policy and then, from July of 1990 onward, as executive vice president for administration, he worked tirelessly, chairing the planning committee, choosing the architect, and creating a team of faculty and senior staff to find answers to funding, space allocation, and other details hashed out in numerous Academic Council meetings. On the Board of Trustees, Dr. George R. Herbert (founding president of the Research Triangle Institute) became our faithful ally early on, lobbying fellow board members and serving as liaison with potential donors, while at the same time demanding of us all plans for a cost-effective structure. Allan Kornberg, a distinguished professor in our Department of Political Science and at the time, chair of the Academic Council, helped us convince the faculty of the importance of the project. His advice proved to be critical as we brought the project to the council for approval before the final trustee vote. In this way the Levine Science Research Center was born to upgrade research space across the campus and to put Medical School investigators side-by-side with science faculty from Trinity College, the School of Engineering, and our new School of the Environment. All saw the importance of enabling the university to recruit and retain excellent scientists who would in turn offer a first-rate education in the sciences to our students in the undergraduate colleges and in our graduate and professional schools. The Medical Center had the cash ready to fund a third of the building, and we were able to get gifts to cover the second third, the largest of which came from Leon Levine, a wonderful supporter of this project. The final third we left to our new president, Nan Keohane, to raise or to fund as my predecessor had funded the new student union, the Bryan Center, when he leveraged Joe Bryan's generous gift with monies from the university's quasi-endowment.

One characteristic that all top-rank research universities can be said to share is a strong faculty role in university governance. It seems to be one of the reliable common denominators of excellence among academic institutions and works no more efficiently there than does democratic governance anywhere else. It is jealously guarded (as it should be) and must be perpetually explained to the trustees (see "Of Cultures and Anarchy," below). Often faculty either despise or distrust the administrator whose curriculum vitae reveals a lack of scholarly achievement and yet, when a scholar takes the helm, it does not necessarily follow that distrust is diminished. Faculty are simultaneously at their best and at their worst in the running of their own institutions—knowledgeable, conscientious, dedicated, they know best how to conduct the education and research enterprise. Nevertheless, in matters of university governance faculty also exhibit—like Congress—a frustrating penchant for academic pork barrelling, reinventing the wheel, and failing to act on their own painstakingly crafted mandates. At Duke examples of the first would include the deans' lobbying of the trustees and much of the opposition to the Levine Center, an illustration of the second would be the academic council's task force on university governance, and of the third the Black Faculty Resolution.

I have noted that among the advantages of entering the Duke presidency by promotion from within was the unique opportunity I had of serving a three-year apprenticeship with a remarkable leader. But having learned so much by virtue of having been inside a prior administration, I suffered the accompanying disadvantage of seeing grudges, disappointments, and suspicions transferred from the old to the new administration—perhaps the inevitable coefficient of the trustees' hoped-for seamless transition from one president to the next. These suspicions led, near the end of 1987, to the Academic Council's decision to appoint a special Task Force on University Governance (soon referred to as TFOG), to explore assertions that the management of the university did not "properly reflect the primacy of teaching and research." At this time there presumably should have been less cause for worries of this kind than is usual among faculty as the presidency had been assumed by one of their own, and the chief academic officer, Provost Phillip Griffiths, was a distinguished scholar from Harvard who had been hired with my full confidence precisely because of his academic stature. In fact, as time passed, the academic credibility of Duke's central administration only increased: with the appointment of Ralph Snyderman to the chancellorship of the Medical Center in 1989 and of Charles Putman as executive vice president for administration (the chief business and finance officer) in 1990, the university was in the unprecedented situation of being run by four James B. Duke professors. This strong academic and research bias among the chief executive officers was maintained when Tom Langford, the William Kellon Quick Professor of Theology and Methodist Studies, agreed to step in as provost in 1991 in the wake of Phillip Griffiths' departure to head the Institute for Advanced Study in Princeton, New Jersey.

Accordingly, with the faculty commitment to excellence in things academic and with the interests of the faculty at heart, Phillip and I had begun immediately to address concerns in the academic sector. Around the time TFOG was created, we had already increased average faculty salaries by 25 percent in the first phase of a process that eventually raised Duke from twelfth to eighth in national rankings of faculty compensation, and we had allocated a larger share of the budget to direct support of scholarship, including library acquisitions, student aid, computing, renovations of classrooms and faculty offices, and the installation of a new telephone system which had the capacity to transmit voice, data, and video text. In addition, as these investments were made, the Capital Campaign for the Arts and Sciences was beginning to endow new chairs that enabled us to expand our faculty with established senior scholars.

The direction of my administration was hardly a secret: from the time I took office until I left, I went about the business of strengthening the faculty. Yet concern persisted among some that they were not sufficiently involved in governance. The irony was that as soon as I became president, I asked for more faculty involvement in administering the university, having worked at Stanford with a model whereby an advisory board was elected from the faculty at large. This body reviewed all appointments, both faculty and administrative, and the overall budget of the university before the president was allowed to submit recommendations on these matters to the board of trustees. When I suggested this model to the Executive Committee of Duke's Academic Council (ECAC), they did not want to change the two-tiered structure we already had in place, wherein ECAC (which was elected by the Academic Council, not by the full faculty) served as the "committee on committees," appointing members of the faculty to the Board of Trustees' committees, to the Administrative Oversight Committee (established in 1982 to advise the chancellor on non-academic matters), and to a variety of other advisory bodies that provided guidance to the provost and the president in such areas as the assignment of academic space, changes in academic budgets, and the recruitment of faculty to establish new programs. Since 1972, as recommended by the Christie Committee (also appointed by the council to reexamine the role of faculty at Duke in university governance), the Academic Council as a whole had been regularly consulted by the administration on plans significantly affecting academic affairs. Most notable in the late seventies had been the discussions in the council related to the retrenchment process carried out under Chancellor Kenneth Pye, which resulted in the termination of the education department and the undergraduate program in the School of Nursing.

TFOG issued an interim report in April of 1988. One of its recommendations was the establishment of a faculty-administration committee on university resources to participate in the development of the budget and advise on policy for allocating resources to our various schools and departments. Despite the inflammatory rhetoric of the report, I was glad to see that this recommendation was consistent with my long-standing desire to involve faculty in the tough decisions about allocating university resources, and I appointed the committee on an interim basis so that the members could begin their work at the start of a budget cycle. When the final, somewhat more constructively written TFOG report was received in January of 1989, I established this committee as a permanent advisory body, added student representatives to its membership, and called it the President's Advisory Committee on Resources (PACOR). I provided it with staff support and instructed the university controller to make available all relevant budget information. Thus, from the faculty point of view, PACOR, whose charge included an annual report to the university community, addressed what had been perceived as an opacity in the administration's approach to budgeting and resource allocation. From the administrative point of view, it responded to my desire for more faculty education about and involvement in university decision making; it reassured the faculty that the president respected their role in governance; and for those who were interested and willing to invest the time, it offered a highly visible avenue for greater understanding of the budget process. I continued to receive from PACOR the kind of advice I had been garnering both as chancellor and president from PACOR's faculty predecessor, the Administrative Oversight Committee, the difference being that AO had been composed solely of faculty and had viewed its mission as examining closely specific items and budgetary concerns, although its charge had not precluded the broad review and analysis of the budget process that PACOR undertook.

The Task Force on University Governance was an internal

matter of little interest outside the walls of Duke University. However, the Black Faculty Resolution—also called the Black Faculty Initiative—became a lightning rod for public controversy both on campus and off, partly because of the political correctness debates but primarily because it addressed a national problem with which our peer institutions were also struggling: the racial imbalance among the faculties at America's research universities. Duke's particular struggles were bracketed by headlines and photos in the *New York Times:* in 1988 when the Black Faculty Initiative was being debated ("Faculty at Duke Is Urged to Hire From Minorities; 500 at Rally on Campus Back Panel Proposal," April 16, p. 6), and on the front page in 1993 when the results were being officially assessed ("Goal Unmet, Duke Reveals Perils In Effort to Increase Black Faculty," September 19). The *Times* saw the issue at Duke as exemplifying affirmative action debates both at universities and in corporate America, and demonstrated the irresistible tendency of the press during the five years of the initiative to focus on the numerical hiring goal we had set. This emphasis misrepresented the key elements of our efforts.

In April of 1988 the Academic Council at Duke debated—and our students, both black and white, rallied—to reach consensus on an effective plan for increasing the number of regular-rank black professors on our faculty. The crux of disagreement during the debate and afterward lay in the rigor of both the goal and the language, "That the Administration *require each hiring unit* within the university [a total of fifty-six] . . . *to increase the number of black faculty* (at regular rank) over its present number . . . *by at least one,* before the fall of 1993" [italics added]. Admittedly this would be difficult, but it was a goal that, as I said at the time, "would distinguish us" from other top-ranked universities and "show that we are making a strong effort here." Opponents of this mandate proposed that a more modest goal be set with an emphasis on encouragements rather than requirements, pointing out that the number of black Ph.D.s in many academic disciplines was minuscule, and arguing that they did not want to be committed to a goal they knew in advance could not be reached. Yet during the debate I supported this mandate that, according to numerous colleagues, was "doomed to failure," and worked hard to implement it throughout my presidency despite persistent public criticism. Why?

First of all, because it was the right thing to do. In the moral sense, it signaled a new attitude, conveyed by the strength of our determination to correct the lingering and still powerful legacies of segregation and Jim Crow. Duke had not been in the vanguard of integration in the South, and it was only just, therefore, that a sense of historical imperative should inform our deliberations. Although a relatively young institution (established in Durham as Trinity College in 1892 and endowed as Duke University in 1924), Duke did not admit blacks to its graduate and professional schools until 1961 nor to its undergraduate colleges until 1963. Thus, for many decades the university had depended on the labor of black workers to maintain its physical plant while denying to their children any opportunity to benefit from a Duke education. Simply complying with federal law in the matter of admissions, i.e., no longer discriminating *against* students on the basis of race, was not enough, especially as Duke, like all private colleges, routinely discriminates in favor of admitting the children of alumni, almost all of whom are white. In this context it seemed both ethical and logical to add race to such other factors as alumni status, gender, geography, athletic ability, musical talent, etc., which we use in selecting students to achieve a balanced class each fall. Similarly, given Duke's historically white professoriate, it seemed at the very least disingenuous not to consider racial diversity a legitimate goal for aggressive faculty recruitment.

In the practical sense, the Black Faculty Initiative was the right thing to do for Duke if we were to maintain our growing reputation, for a significant black presence is absolutely necessary at a research university. It is necessary in order to erode the body of prejudice within a predominantly white student population who benefit greatly from exposure in the classroom to black professors like historian John Hope Franklin and to black students who can offer points of view forged by a lifetime of exposure to subtle and not-so-subtle racial bigotry; to provide role models for the black students we recruit and for younger black scholars; to present a more welcoming aspect to people of color who come to institutions like Duke from around the world for study, research, and advanced training; and to develop some of the newer fields of knowledge that are minority specific and which therefore have tended to attract a higher proportion of minority scholars. For example, at Duke Medical Center the major studies in sickle-cell anemia have been run primarily by black faculty, and in the arts and sciences African American history and culture have been neglected by the white majority.

Second, I supported the 1988 Black Faculty Initiative because, far from being "naive and unrealistic" as it was dubbed in the local press, the plan itself contained the answer to the greatest difficulty in meeting the goal: it aimed to increase the small pool of black faculty candidates by training more black graduate students. To do this, we created programs to attract black graduate and professional school students and we hired a full-time recruiter for the graduate school. This strategy proved to be the real success story of the resolution, for although the net gain in regular-rank black faculty from the fall of 1987 to the fall of 1993 was discouragingly small—only eight, from thirty-one to thirty-nine—we more than doubled the number of black doctoral candidates enrolled at Duke, from twenty-one to fifty-two, with a commensurate increase in funding to support them, from $293,201 to $786,730. This was one of the goals of the resolution and facilitated the hiring goal, providing the long-term solution for Duke and for other research universities as well. It is regrettable that resistance among the faculty to hiring our own graduate students prevented us from making the most of this aspect of the plan, a course of action I argued strongly for during the debate.

The third reason I supported the 1988 resolution was that the second phase of the initiative contained a provision that added teeth to the plan: in 1993 departments that had not appointed at least one black scholar to their tenured or tenure-track faculty ranks would be required to submit new recruitment plans for approval by the equal employment opportunity officer and the appropriate dean before any further faculty could be recruited by the department. It was disappointing, therefore, that when the time came for invoking this administrative sanction in the fall of 1993, the original 1988 resolution was declared a failure both in the press and among some campus constituencies and the second phase was never implemented. Instead, the following January a new resolution was approved by the Academic Council, calling for the total number of black faculty at Duke to be doubled over the course of ten years. I was glad to see, however, that this renewed initiative of 1994 built on the tenets and the lessons of the previous resolution, spelling out in even greater detail strategies to be used in recruiting and increasing the pool; calling for stricter monitoring and disincentives; and pointing out the importance of mentoring and of providing a collegial and supportive, nonracist atmosphere, something I had also addressed in my 1993 report to the faculty on the progress of the original resolution (see "The Benchmarks of Community," below).

A fourth reason I supported the 1988 plan was Duke history, which had taught me that encouragement and financial incentives unaccompanied by the twin pressures of faculty-approved goals and administrative monitoring yielded only modest, if any, success. When I came to Duke in 1974 efforts to increase black faculty in the arts and sciences chiefly through establishing a black studies program had made little progress. For a variety of reasons—inexperience, inadequate funding, faculty disinterest, confusion about how to proceed—the program remained weak, and while the number of black faculty had increased slightly since its inception in 1969, from one to six, only one of these professors was tenured. Not surprisingly, when, in response to expressed student concerns, Terry Sanford created the President's Council on Black Affairs in November of 1975, the council's first report recommended that administrative action be taken specifically to encourage departments to hire more black faculty. Thus was born the incentives plan unfortunately called for many years the "add-on policy" and which, as chancellor, I inherited. Simply stated, the policy constituted a pledge by the administration to fund the appointment of black scholars by departments and schools (excepting the Medical School) regardless of whether a vacancy existed. Nevertheless, despite this addition of financial fuel to good intentions, from the announcement of the policy in the fall of 1976 by Provost Frederic Cleaveland to the spring of 1982, when I was appointed chancellor, the number of tenured or tenure-track black faculty in the arts and sciences increased by only one, from six to seven—and this despite the leadership of Provost Bill Bevan, who was instrumental in hiring two very distinguished black scholars.

To be overcome, institutional inertia in matters of race must be attacked with vigor by every constituency. In the six years preceding the 1988 resolution at Duke, the Board of Trustees, Terry Sanford, and I had joined with the Academic Council in providing affirmative action leadership, articulating goals, and developing strategies for increasing the number of black faculty at Duke. We had some success: from the fall of 1983 to the fall of 1984 the total number of black faculty at regular rank increased from twenty-two to thirty-one. Yet, despite this momentum, the demonstrated supportiveness of the administration, and the continuing involvement of the Academic Council both as a body and as individuals, the faculty at large remained uncommitted, simply saying, when queried, that "no blacks applied," or that there were none in the pool. In the spring of 1985 the Academic Council passed, with only one dissenting vote, the recommendation that we double the number of black faculty at Duke by 1989/1990; in the fall of 1986 the chair of the council's Committee on Black Faculty, Professor Robert Osborn, reported that in the first year of this renewed commitment the number of black faculty at Duke had actually fallen from twenty-eight to twenty-seven, and after reviewing the efforts of a number of departments, he and the committee

> had to conclude that not every department is working as hard at it as are other departments, and that the problem right now is not with the administration. One of the main charges to this committee was to monitor the administration, but what I think is becoming clear is that we are going to have to monitor the faculty perhaps a little more closely than we are the administration.

Professor Osborn's comments highlight what I found to be one of the constant problems in implementing affirmative action goals at a university: the administration is always held accountable—responsible for hiring more black faculty—when it is the faculty themselves at the departmental level who control the process. Faculty committees identify fields of knowledge in which scholars are needed, place ads in the professional publications, contact colleagues at other institutions, review candidates, and so forth. This is as it should be, but interestingly, our Academic Council at Duke has often called for the administration to develop lists of potential black faculty or hire a person especially designated to accomplish this task for the various schools and departments. I have never been sanguine about such a measure, wondering why the schools and departments should pay any attention to the recommendations of someone outside their own disciplines. One of the most important things any administration can do—earmark special funds for minority hires—we did do at Duke, and for that we were roundly criticized by numerous faculty who saw these monies as "buying blacks" to the detriment of the salaries of professors already serving the institution loyally. Yet such complaints are seldom voiced, or if voiced, are not so vociferously expressed, when economic realities lead to higher salaries for professional school faculty and those in areas of scholarship where the supply of faculty is scarce. Thus it was the case that the president and the administration were faulted by the faculty for not doing what the faculty would never dream of allowing us to do—make unilateral hires—and for doing what we could do—spend money on extra positions or competitive hires.

This, then, is some of the background to what may have seemed to outsiders the extreme nature of the 1988 resolution at Duke. Despite the high profile of our initiative and the commitment expressed by the Academic Council, the fact was that there was little interest among the general faculty for pursuing the mandate. Our subsequent five years of sincere efforts were, I believe, seriously damaged by constant public criticisms of the policy because they contributed to a perception that Duke was an unfriendly place for black scholars. On the other hand, the call for recruiting and supporting more black graduate students, the most promising element of the 1988 resolution, led to real progress at Duke in producing the Ph.D.'s who are the black professoriate of the future; and the reports of the standing Committee on Black Faculty and the discussions of those reports in council as the new mandate is monitored should continue to engender the good ideas and practical approaches we began developing during our controversial deliberations of 1988.

In the last two decades it has become commonplace to state that university presidents do not have nearly the power they used to have. Whether this is true or not I cannot say; it may be that nowadays similar amounts of power are still being exercised, but in dissimilar ways. Based on my own experience, I can delineate some clear avenues of power that are generally open to presidents of private research universities.

First, a lot of presidential effort should go into recognizing academic talent and supporting it. This is done by looking for ways to attract or retain intellectual leaders who are generating exciting scholarship in new areas of knowledge or who are approaching established fields of study in innovative ways, and supporting their recruitment or retention by a dean or department chair. This effort usually involves providing additional funds, space, equipment, or library holdings, and in some cases, employment for spouses or domestic partners. The Levine Science Research Center was in part conceived to attract and hold stellar faculty—scientists and engineers committed to addressing important research problems such as contamination of the world environment, the search for more effective treatment and prevention of cancer and AIDS, and the contributions of new technology to the international economy. Perhaps it would be accurate to generalize that my own exercise of presidential power became more than anything else a matter of choosing to strengthen targeted areas for academic growth at Duke while adding a few that were new. Other presidents focus on sustaining an institution through growth by substitution (for every new program initiated an "old" program is discontinued) or through the selective elimination of existing programs in order to sustain what is left. Fortunately, Duke had already taken this bitter medicine prior to my presidency, having retrenched during the late seventies and early eighties.

The addition of new programs or the enhancement of existing programs requires that new money be identified, and this is why fundraising is a second avenue of presidential power and such an important part of the job. Duke was extremely fortunate in having Joel Fleishman to direct the Capital Campaign for the Arts and Sciences—a directorship Terry had talked him into taking in 1982

—and John Piva to oversee our development efforts university wide, including the running of our central office, which involved clearance and record keeping. Both these senior vice presidents proved remarkably successful, yet clearly there were fundraising chores that could be done only by the president. For example, a private lunch with Ross Johnson, CEO of RJR Nabisco, brought in $4 million, funding two endowed professorships and part of a building; a series of personal conversations with Dave Thomas of Wendy's brought another $4 million to establish an executive education program at Duke's Fuqua School of Business. A trip to Erie, Pennsylvania, resulted several years later in a gift of $12 million in endowment money from the Thomas Lord Foundation. Many donors and development officers felt that million-dollar gifts required presidential involvement. Sometimes this was the case and I enjoyed the "ask." In some other notable instances the president was not involved, as with Joe Bryan's gift of $10 million for our neurobiology building. This extraordinary contribution was solicited by Dr. Allen Roses, head of neurology at Duke, and by Dr. William Anlyan, our chancellor for health affairs, who were trusted by the donor—a trust developed over years of friendship. Fortunately, Duke was an easy university to promote with donors—everyone wanted to support a rising star. The highly visible success of the basketball team offered a bridge to involving potential donors in support of our academic programs, and so I used the power of basketball tickets judiciously, distributing regular season, tournament, and Final Four tickets to VIP's with the good of the institution in mind. These games were not recreational events for me, but rather key opportunities for intensive fundraising—days and nights of breakfasts, lunches, dinners, and trustee-hosted parties where I talked with alumni and potential benefactors, ate as little as possible, and heard everybody's complaints about their stadium seats. But it paid off: gifts came to the university with such increasing magnitude and frequency that by the time I left the presidency the endowment had more than doubled and annual voluntary support had tripled, from approximately $40 million in 1984 to over $140 million in 1993. Duke moved from twenty-first to seventh in overall gifts among public and private universities and acquired the reputation of being able to afford new ventures.

Integral to the successful exercise of presidential influence in both these spheres—targeting areas of growth and fundraising—is the matter of leadership style. There must be a match between the philosophy of the leader on the one hand and the institution and the times on the other. Terry Sanford had been an aggressive public figure whose political skills served Duke well, bringing the institution into the national limelight and building the strong alumni network this relatively young university needed for financial stability. The mission of my succeeding presidency was to foster solid internal growth and strategic risk taking. I realized, though, that a research university is far too complex an entity—too filled with individual and maverick genius—to achieve dramatic change under conditions of authoritarian control and micromanagement. Accordingly, as chancellor, provost, and president, my leadership style was synergistic; that is, I delegated leadership in specific spheres to others who had demonstrated capacities for achievement. I then gave credit to them for change, having relied on my psychiatric skills to make effective administrative appointments. Paramount among the personality traits I was seeking in my appointees were altruism, a commitment to team effort and hard work, a sense of institutional loyalty, integrity, and the ability to nurture and mentor others. I gave these officers and deans my support within the constraints of available resources, and encouraged them to create and sustain excellence in their areas of responsibility. My support included funds; help with fundraising by approaching corporations, foundations, and individuals; and help with recruiting faculty by hosting luncheons and dinners and telephoning when appropriate. I was most comfortable with this leadership style—cooperative, supportive, giving full credit to others for their achievements—and it proved to be effective for Duke, where we were fortunate in having a large pool of world-class talent among the faculty. I relied on their advice in charting new territories for university involvement, realizing that as a physician I was not well versed in the recent developments in most fields outside the Medical Center. I trusted the judgment of those appointed to lead the academic units and rarely was that trust misplaced: between 1982 and 1993 Duke's academic standing improved dramatically, as gauged by the National Research Council's surveys of research-doctorate programs in the United States (the most respected measure of quality among American research universities). Whereas in 1982 Duke had only nine departments in the top twenty with two of those in the top ten, the 1993 survey placed eighteen of our departments in the top twenty with eight in the top ten.[3] The results of a policy of strong academic leadership backed by an increased flow of resources were most striking in the humanities, where five departments (comparative literature, English, French, religion, and Spanish) ranked in the top ten. In fact, the rise of the English department from 28 to 5.5 (indicating a tie with Stanford for fifth place) was sufficiently notable to make the front page of the *New*

3. Ranked in the top twenty in 1982 were biochemistry (14.5), botany (11), cell and molecular biology (16.5), classics (18), French (14.5), physiology (9), political science (18), Spanish (18), zoology (5.5); in 1993, anthropology (18.5), biochemistry and molecular biology (15), biomedical engineering (4), cell and developmental biology (14), classics (15), comparative literature (2), ecology, evolution, and behavior (3), English (5.5), French (3), history (15), molecular and general genetics (15), neurosciences (16.5), oceanography (13.5), pharmacology (5), political science (14), religion (4), sociology (20), Spanish (2). See *An Assessment of Research-Doctorate Programs in the United States*, ed. Lyle V. Jones, Gardner Lindzey, and Porter E. Coggeshall (Washington, D.C.: National Academy Press, 1982) and *Research-Doctorate Programs in the United States: Continuity and Change*, ed. Marvin L. Goldberger, Brendan A. Maher, and Pamela Ebert Flattau (Washington, D.C.: National Academy Press, 1995).

York Times.[4] The release of the new NRC rankings in the fall of 1995 was for me a joyous and fulfilling moment, one of those rare occasions when a president can see clear-cut returns on years of strenuous efforts to achieve the ultimate academic intangible—a measurable increase in the intellectual quality of the faculty. My goal had been to lead Duke University to the next level of excellence among its peer institutions, and more than two years after stepping down, I was more than happy to receive at last the news of our success.

Perhaps this is the point at which to acknowledge the obvious: my leadership style is inextricably bound up with my background as a psychiatrist, a factor that was never diluted in the eleven years I served as chancellor and president of Duke. The listening, reactive side of me served the institution in large ways and small. Listening first and then acting always seemed to me the surest route to building consensus or defusing a crisis in the making, though it is not a quick-fix administrative tool. There must be a long-term investment in slowing down every day and hearing what people have to say about what they are thinking, feeling, or wondering. I tried to weave this practice into my administrative style so thoroughly that, in the end, it went virtually unremarked. The president's open office hours for students, open office door for faculty, reliable and active presence at Academic Council meetings—all of these were, I believe, taken for granted by the university community. While chancellor, at the request of the Academic Council, I had instituted a question-and-answer period at each council meeting during which faculty could query me, and later Provost Griffiths, on any subject. As president I continued this custom faithfully because I recognized the desirability of having the president there and accessible, willing to listen and to discuss any issue, confirming that the admin-

4. William H. Honan, "Study of Graduate Programs Serves Up Several Surprises," *New York Times*, Sept. 13, 1995, A1, B8.

istration had nothing to hide. In the first few years I handled all the questions myself, but as these frequently involved such varied staff-of-life matters as parking or phone rates or the lack of availability of basketball tickets, I began to find it was more valuable to ask the officer or individual responsible for a particular area to attend the meeting also and help respond to follow-up questions. Eventually, toward the end of my eight years as president, the questions grew fewer and fewer, such that in my last year only two questions were submitted.

Interestingly, this gradual decline was paralleled among the students, for whom the President's Suggestion Box was opened with great fanfare in the student center. At first we received stacks of little cards filled out by students, which drove the staff crazy because I insisted that anyone who had the courtesy to sign the card and provide an address deserved an answer. Therefore, the relevant person in the institution (including me) responded to each of the queries, which were usually quite interesting and sometimes very helpful. There were well over 100 suggestions the first year, but gradually the rate of suggestions trickled off. In my last year as president we would send our work-study student over to open the box only to find that it contained a few particles of dust but no cards.

The psychology in both these cases lies, I think, in the natural desire to test the system—for a faculty member, to test the president with a difficult question in the public venue of a council meeting; for a student, to find out if the president really would respond seriously to a "mere" undergraduate. Once it became known that the president was well informed on the topics of the day and would indeed get up and address the issue or write back, then interest naturally waned. Also, I think the institution calmed down over the years of my presidency. It may have had to do with students becoming less restive; it may have had to do with faculty beginning to see their compensation and benefits increasing and their comparative ranking in salary improving each year. Buildings were refurbished and computers were upgraded and the library got more space and holdings. All of this activity continually sent the message that the president was listening and the administration was acting, doing exactly what one trustee had stated so well—"Dr. Brodie, you are bringing Duke up to the level of its reputation!"

A fourth avenue of power for university presidents is the front page of the local newspaper, and it is an avenue I found to be riddled with potholes. As the CEO of the second largest private employer in the state, I certainly realized I would be listened to beyond the Duke campus. The press's spotlight on everything Duke-related is understandable. Most of our employees are drawn from the local community, and matters pertaining to their welfare quite naturally occupy a significant amount of daily newsprint just as they occupied a significant amount of my time. I found that where the press was concerned I had a fairly large megaphone, but this proved to be both an opportunity and a hazard, as a discouraging number of comments were taken out of context, misunderstood, or reported inaccurately or incompletely. In addition, as a scientist, physician, and educator, I was unprepared for the lack of research and objectivity that marked much of the news coverage of Duke.

One theme in particular resonated with the press: the Durham community seemed always to want more of the university than the university was perceived to be giving. This desire was relentlessly communicated via hundreds of column inches primarily in the Durham *Herald-Sun*, where Duke was portrayed as an "ivory tower" that had all the answers. If only the inhabitants of the tower would come down and help Durham address crime in the streets, problems in the schools, heavy tax burdens, the quality of the water, and the quality of life—if only we at Duke would drop for a while our focus on the rest of the world and focus instead on Durham, then these problems would go away. I knew, of course, that similar coverage was being afforded universities in other local newspapers in the 1980s as the denizens of city hall eyed the resources of the colleges and universities in their midst. But this did little to lessen the sting of undeserved criticisms at home. Those at Duke who could help were already doing so, and the state of knowledge available to address human problems of community was in part contributed to by Duke faculty as well as faculty at every other research university in America. We did not have magic answers to local problems; if we had, we surely would have shared them. And despite the tenor of columns and editorials chiding Duke, we *were* sharing with Durham in a host of ways that went far beyond the employer-employee relationship: we heavily promoted Durham's annual United Way campaign within Duke and offered the option of payroll deductions; we provided a revolving $1.2 million low-income housing loan fund; our Medical Center provided $30 million and more in free care each year to citizens of Durham County and surrounding areas; our basketball teams visited local classrooms to impress on youngsters the importance of reading; we set up a community service center, and by the time I left office, over half of our graduating seniors had volunteered in Durham neighborhoods, schools, and soup kitchens.

I myself took community service very seriously and always had. Certainly my seven years on the Area Mental Health Board of Durham County which I chaired in 1981–82 had been rewarding and taught me much about my new home. Local public service is important for university presidents: it clarifies and smooths town-gown relations as the president comes into frequent contact with civic leaders, and it sets an example, encouraging others in the university to participate, especially students, for whom volunteer work in the local community serves important educational purposes. As is usual among university presidents, some of my service was as a trustee of not-for-profit organizations through which I could help to advance the broad economic and educational interests of our region. These board memberships included the Microelectronics Center of North Carolina, the Research Triangle Institute, the Research Triangle Foundation, and the Commission on the Future of North Carolina's Community College System. Within Duke I led numerous Durham initiatives by our students, faculty, and staff, helping to found Project BUILD through which hundreds of Duke students have aided the homeless of Durham; providing computers and a van to a student-led tutorial program for Durham children; establishing programs specifically aimed at supporting the Durham schools, including designating a Duke vice president as liaison with the schools; and mandating involvement in civic affairs when I hired a vice president to head our newly created division of public affairs. I responded to requests to serve on panels sponsored by the Durham Human Relations Commission and the county commissioners; I met with both the county commissioners and the city council whenever new members were elected; and for a year I made the time to meet monthly with the principal, business manager, and faculty leaders of Durham High School. I helped recruit a new school superintendent and a new chief of police. The needs of Durham—charitable, civic, and cultural—were acknowledged in thousands of hours donated by Duke officers, faculty, staff, and students, and in tens of thousands of dollars in direct contributions from Duke to Durham.

Nevertheless, despite the millions of dollars pumped into the Durham economy each year as a result of Duke's presence, the stability and high quality of the employment we offer to our largely Durham-based workforce, my continuous involvement, and the efforts of the university community to be responsible, generous, and creative citizens, throughout my presidency the newspapers harped on the assertion that Duke was turning its back on Durham and not contributing to the solution of metropolitan problems. What could I or any of us at Duke do in the face of this persistent railing? In the end I discovered, almost inadvertently, the power of the president's megaphone when I paid a visit to the Durham Rotary Club. There I delivered a speech about what I thought Durham should be doing to solve its own problems, a talk which I quite frankly considered out of character for me in its prescriptive nature and critical tone. The next morning, to my surprise, I discovered myself in a positive story on the front page of the local paper, described as having been "warmly received" by civic leaders who had responded favorably to my judgment that our city was "adrift and inefficient"! That day's editorial praised me for "insightful comments about the city's festering social and economic problems"; the somewhat oversized editorial cartoon (six-by-eight inches) depicted me as a benign psychiatrist prescribing merger for Durham city and county's "Multiple Personality Disorder"; and a highly complimentary column in the following Sunday's edition commended me for "the most direct words you've heard on city politics in a long time." This unaccustomed praise was appreciated, if surprising; for whatever reason, it appeared that press criticisms of Duke could be deflected by more frequent, direct, even critical comments by me on the state of our community, and I concluded that in the past I had been too sparing with my use of the unpredictable power of the president's megaphone.

The final lever of presidential power I would cite is one that the president must use or risk losing credibility both on campus and off. I am speaking of the university president's "bully pulpit," the expectation that the leader of an academic institution will speak out with some measure of informed judgment on moral or ethical questions and social issues. I believe that this expectation is not unreasonable. Those who lead research universities are not the possessors of superhuman wisdom but are privileged to have daily access to more of what is currently known and thought in more fields of knowledge than those in any other occupational group. It is therefore not surprising that in the eyes of the public, university presidents are seen as empowered by the institutions they serve. For me, this perception had its lighter side—chiefly the daily mail which brought requests from all over the country for advice on everything from reading lists to recipes—but more often I felt the responsibility of the office to weigh in on important public issues, especially as they touched on the concerns of educators. When I was asked to speak to groups outside the university on a loosely defined topic or with no topic defined at all (always a more difficult assignment), I used the opportunity to address a pertinent ethical dilemma or to highlight an area of inequity in our society. In Madrid, for example, I explained the steps we had taken at Duke to safeguard the ethics of university-industry research relationships (see "Tradition and Progress," below); on Girls and Women in Sports Day I used my role as the nominal host of this annual event to call statewide attention to the troubling decline in the number of women in coaching (see "Girls and Women in Sports," below). I came to the defense of the idea of a university whenever alumni, donors, or the press applied pressures that could stifle academic freedom, as happened during the height of the anti-p.c. frenzy (see, for example, "In Defense of Professors," below), or might deprive the university of the right to make a moral decision, as happened in the spring of 1986 when Duke decided to sell its stock in companies doing business in South Africa. And sometimes it even became necessary for me to take on local town-gown tensions and defend universities' special role in society and the principles that protect that role, as cities all over the country began attacking the tax-exempt status of higher education, hoping to pick nonprofit pockets in the name of curing urban ills.

On campus it was clearly one of the duties of the president to respond frequently to trustee, faculty, and student requests to speak on a variety of occasions, most of which seemed inevitably to require a discussion of values—the values to which universities are committed and which trustees must learn to share, the values that define collegiality among a faculty if intellectual community is to flourish, the values a student athlete should strive to represent, and the values college students should carry with them when they graduate (all topics represented by speeches in this volume). Undeniably, there is an almost daily pastoral element to a presidency that must be exercised publicly as well as privately. Far less often—but much more dramatic—are the campus controversies and crises when even relatively brief public statements by the president carry great symbolic value. Among such instances at Duke I recall the apology I tendered on behalf of the university community to our food service workers, who had been slandered in a misguided student effort at satire; the statement of support for the student editors who agonized over whether to publish a Holocaust revisionists' ad in our campus newspaper, the *Chronicle* (see the introduction to "The Tools of Democracy," below); the memorandum I circulated to the other presidents of Atlantic Coast Conference universities, calling for an official protest of the notorious "Girls of the A.C.C." issue of *Playboy*.

Of course, public criticism as well as public support comes with taking these positions, though such criticism is hardly painful when it consists of being singled out for ridicule in the editorial pages of a publication like *Playboy*. More difficult is the conflict with faculty who feel the president has no "right" to express a view because that view will be taken as representing "the view" of the entire university. However, as long as the viewpoint is clearly labeled as the personal opinion of the president, it is far better that he or she be heard. Certainly, presidents who do not take strong public stands do not last long; the board chair or the provost or a vice president will step forward to fill the vacuum in more ways than one. Faculty who disagree with a president's statements have access to a number of powerful public venues to express their opinions, including newspapers, campus rallies, and faculty councils. Further, the consequences of presidents' *not* speaking for the record often constitute an abandonment of those within our institutions who may feel vulnerable—the young women who felt degraded by blatant newspaper ads soliciting female Duke students to pose nude, the student editors who suffered withering public criticism after making a difficult call, the employees who felt that their daily labor to make our campus an inviting community was not respected. In such cases the self-image of individuals and entire groups can be undermined by a presidential silence or uplifted by a statement of support. In corporate life top-down leadership has long been recognized as essential to effecting policy or attitude changes in a company; the same is demonstrably true in higher education, and I kept in mind always the powerful agents of change my own words and actions could be. That is why the "bully pulpit" is an element in every one of the speeches collected here, for as an educator I ultimately concluded that few speeches are worth making if some question of principle is not being addressed.

2

ASSESSING OUR ROLE

The Inaugural Address

In the 1970s and early '80s it had become fashionable in academia to lambaste all of big business for the profit mongering and gross corporate indiscretions that had been discovered through Congressional inquiry. As long as I was president of Duke, in fact, it continued to be the case that many faculty saw corporate America as an enemy to be attacked and criticized and held accountable, and not to be seen in any way as a partner in educating and nurturing bright young minds and new talent.

But during the latter half of the 1980s corporate gifts to higher education for the first time began to exceed giving by charitable foundations. Naturally, I wanted to position Duke to receive an increasing share of these funds. After all, our colleges and universities produce most of the people who go into executive and middle-management positions in business and industry and all of the scientists and engineers who conduct the research and development efforts in corporate laboratories. And the fact was, corporate America had not been paying its dues. Furthermore, I wanted to boost our youngest school at Duke, the Fuqua School of Business, which had graduated its first class only thirteen years before. Accordingly, I brought in new corporate leaders to serve on our Board of Trustees—R. David Thomas of Wendy's, George Grune of Reader's Digest, Susan King of Corning, Randall Tobias of AT&T, F. Ross Johnson of RJR-Nabisco, Roy Bostock of D'Arcy Masius Benton & Bowles, John Koskinen of Palmieri & Company, Ernie Mario of Glaxo, and Eugene Patterson of the St. Petersburg Times. *With their help and with the efforts of officers and staff throughout the university and Medi-*

cal Center, Duke's annual share of corporate gifts went from $10.9 million in 1984 to $53.4 million in 1993 (not counting contract income), an increase of 388 percent. By the time I stepped down we had gone from eighteenth to second among universities reporting corporate giving, and our business school, under the leadership of Dean Thomas Keller and with the continuing involvement and support of business leaders like J. B. Fuqua and R. David Thomas, had gained national recognition.

As I contemplated the need for America's universities to join in closer partnership with American business, I knew the times demanded that we address the complicated issues raised by apartheid and the dilemma of firms doing business in South Africa. Duke had not yet decided whether to continue to hold stock in those firms, but over the subsequent six months, faculty, students, staff, and trustees came to a determination. On May 6, 1986, the Board of Trustees voted to divest because we felt it was time to send a strong message that apartheid was unacceptable under any conditions, not only to the individuals involved, but also to Duke University. This action resulted in a year or so of angry letters from corporate supporters and some withdrawn pledges, but ultimately, almost everyone who withdrew support renewed it well before 1994 when the board reversed the divestment decision after apartheid had been abolished.

THE INAUGURAL ADDRESS OF H. KEITH H. BRODIE, M.D.
SEVENTH PRESIDENT OF DUKE UNIVERSITY
SEPTEMBER 28, 1985

We have come together here today because we are proud of this place. We are proud of what has been accomplished here, and we are proud of our hopes for the future. Our history in this place is not long, and there is some advantage to that, for we can still trace this university to individual, private efforts. We can name names. We can recall the words of agreements, bequests, and resolutions. We remember the day when a great school began to stir.

There is a wonderful sense of continuity for us here. In these ceremonies we reach back to a sense of this place as it was envisioned for us one lifetime ago. In today's rituals we seek our connection with the past and reassurance that what we are about here does matter, that we are doing the right thing. When people had no words they acted out in rituals what was, for them, inexpressible. Perhaps hopes for the future are, ultimately, inexpressible. Perhaps by investing these moments with formality and beauty, our human ritual and remembrance, we can conjure the future.

Such a fanciful notion may have been abroad that autumn day seventy-five years ago when William Preston Few was inaugurated as president of Trinity College. He had hopes already, intimations of the future, encouraged by the generosity and idealism of Julian S. Carr and the Duke family. By what wonderful ceremony was that occasion marked, as though everyone firmly believed that the braver the beginning, the more certain their success. The retiring president, John Carlisle Kilgo, had been a good leader for the college, but in the previous summer in Asheville he was elected to the office of bishop of the Methodist Episcopal Church, South. It was decided that the inauguration of Trinity's new president should not take place before the dedication of the Washington Duke Building, and so the two events were combined for an even grander celebration. The gala ended around eleven o'clock that night, when the students of Trinity College marched with lanterns and torches to the home of Mr. and Mrs. Benjamin Newton Duke on Chapel Hill Street. There, students serenaded the Dukes and their guests, friends and faculty of the college.[1]

I am struck by the exuberance of that celebration, by the tremendous confidence and enthusiasm of all the participants. It is as though by acting joyfully on that occasion they were predicting the future. We know now that they were justified in their ex-

1. Introduction to *The Inauguration of William Preston Few as President of Trinity College* (Durham, N.C.: [Trinity College], Nov. 9, 1910).

traordinary spirit of pride and affection. From that day forward the growth of Duke University proved to be phenomenal. As one historian has noted, the campus of old Trinity College became the site of a "greater transformation . . . in a shorter space of time, than had ever occurred [in the history of higher education] in the South."[2]

Taking over the leadership of a good, small college that day in 1910, President Few envisioned for it a strong role in the Southern region, and that role he defined in terms of the place and the times. The "Southern people are poor," he stated bluntly. They were still suffering in the aftermath of the Civil War and Reconstruction, and the "chaotic" conditions of the South's public school system, he further pointed out, had yet to be put right. The duty of Trinity College was clear: to train, through the study of the liberal arts, men and women who would perform their civic responsibilities with "courage and moral energy," who would bring both "efficiency and character" to producing wealth for an impoverished region, and as an institution, to lead in uplifting and reforming the racially dual public school system of the state. "I have sought to emphasize my belief," he said, "that our colleges should give themselves to the doing of the hard tasks of society. . . ."[3]

Today much of the South is no longer impoverished, and Duke University strongly occupies its place in what is arguably the fastest growing, most prosperous region in the country. The times and the tasks of our society have changed, but our duty to take them on has not. Courage and moral energy are still needed

2. Robert H. Woody, "William Preston Few: A Biographical Appreciation," in *The Papers and Addresses of William Preston Few* (Durham, N.C.: Duke University Press, 1951), p. 107.

3. William Preston Few, "The Inaugural Address," in *The Inauguration of William Preston Few*, pp. 48–50.

in carrying out our responsibilities to the world; character and efficiency are still wanted for the leaders of our nation's business and industry. Today I would identify these goals once again as our especial tasks. To achieve them, we should recognize Duke's potential for leadership in several areas.

First, we must work hard to engender mutual respect between corporate America and our academic institutions. Recently, Donald Rumsfeld, former U.S. secretary of defense, identified the problem. Sometime in the 1950s, says Rumsfeld, the United States became an " 'adversarial society,' where rather than wishing the enterprise system well, [academia] vacillated between neutrality and hostility."[4] He noted that at times the academic community demonstrated an attitude of downright disrespect toward the world of business. This alienation developed momentum in the 1960s and '70s, when some universities tended to foster the notion that there was something necessarily crass in a business career.

Now we have reached a time when we have become a debtor nation, when we are told that America's debt to foreign nations will reach $1 trillion in 1990; a time when foreign apparel is flooding our marketplace and our balance of trade even in microelectronics is negative. With all these indicators, the American free enterprise system needs our support. As Rumsfeld puts it, comparing American support for commerce with that found in Japan, "If you have two racers, and on one side people are encouraging one and wishing him well, and on the other side they are putting weights on the racer and heaving tomatoes at him, one ought not be surprised that the race comes out the way it has."[5]

The American free enterprise system needs its universities.

4. Donald H. Rumsfeld, "American Leadership in World Affairs," *Princeton Alumni Weekly*, March 13, 1985, 23.
5. Rumsfeld, 23.

American business needs the knowledge we can generate and the young people we are preparing. And we need the fruits of healthy commerce. History teaches us that times of economic success are associated with an age of creativity in the arts and sciences. It was no coincidence that the great artists of the Renaissance frequently painted the portraits of a prosperous merchant class, or that Shakespeare wrote thirty-seven of the greatest plays in the English language for a paying audience. The rise of the novel in the nineteenth century was a direct result of the Industrial Revolution, which produced a class of people who had the leisure and the money to learn to read and to buy books. What a terrible burden it is to our students whose gifts are commercial, rather than poetic or scientific, to imply that somehow their contribution to society will be less than that of others; how wrongheaded even to suggest that what they are able to do best is not the best thing for them to do.

Society's interests are rightly served by business, just as they are served by education, by government, by science, by technology, by literature and music and art. It is important to America that this university produce leaders in all these realms—leaders, as President Few observed, who shall do their chosen work with character and efficiency, with courage and moral energy. For some time now many thoughtful students who might want to enter the mainstream of commerce have shied away, have hesitated for fear that the profit motive is somehow not honorable. But the generation of capital is a proper end if it benefits society at large, and it is a proper means to an end if it enables the individual to do charitable works, to support the church, to contribute to the arts, and to sustain those who are less fortunate throughout the world.

Surely, commitment to a free enterprise system, to a passion for excellence and hard work, to upward mobility through education, to the promise of America—hallmarks of corporate values today—surely these are worthy characteristics. I hope it can be said of this university that it seeks to inspire these values in all who come to learn in this place and that our students keep these virtues for a lifetime.

But these are not the only values Duke University seeks to transmit. We shall not produce narrowly educated, vocationally trained graduates, but we shall send forth men and women who are broadly educated in the arts and sciences. For commerce needs people who have the proper humane values, who see profit in perspective, who know that cost-benefit analysis will not solve the increasing ethical dilemmas of high technology and world trade. American business will not prosper by taking the short view, either in research and development or in people. The university is a place where new knowledge is developed and where people are developed as well—people who can think through the implications for the future because they have gained the perspective which only a strong liberal arts background can give them, a historical perspective, an ethical perspective.

I can offer you no better example of the worldwide complexities that have increased the need of American business for broadly educated leaders than the tragic situation in South Africa. There, corporations face daily an agonizing moral dilemma: should they continue economic participation in a society that denies basic human rights to the majority of its people? Should, for example, McGraw-Hill book company withdraw from South Africa, taking with it the money and influence that helped to establish the only bookstore in the all-black South African city of Soweto, within walking distance of many of Soweto's youngsters, who need books and school supplies? Should Borden Milk withdraw, thus diminishing by one-third the supply of milk in South Africa, milk necessary to the diets of rural black children from the age of eighteen months to five years? These are dramatic examples, I admit, but I offer them because it is tempting in such situations to view issues as clear-cut when they are not. When is a principle more important than individual lives? When is a principle best served in terms of individual lives?

I know that the right way is hard to find, for this university has also struggled with great issues of freedom and right when the way was not clear. Long ago a member of our faculty spoke out for equal citizenship for black people, and for his forthrightness brought down on this institution nothing less than the threat of extinction. In that struggle, known as the Bassett Affair, this school established for all time the principle of academic freedom, the principle that says professors shall not be penalized for speaking their beliefs. But that principle was ensured to the nation by endangering an entire community of individual scholars.

I believe that, for the most part, American business is struggling in good faith with questions like that of South Africa just as this university once struggled to do the right thing in support of Professor Bassett. We are proud of that decision, and our sense of pride is important, as Terry Sanford has pointed out, because it "helps us to face other [such] decisions more courageously."[6] We still debate the hard questions here, and we actively engage our students in those debates as part of their necessary preparation for life in what many outside the university like to refer to as the "real world." I suggest that American universities and American business are both seeking right action for the same world and that we should acknowledge more often that we are friends of the same demanding road.

The chaotic conditions in other parts of the world remind us that seventy-five years ago this institution felt the most urgent needs lay here, where the chaotic conditions of the South's public school system endangered Southern society by hampering the development of a well-informed, responsible citizenry. The re-

6. President Terry Sanford, "On Doing the Right Thing" (presented at a meeting of the Academic Council, Duke University, Dec. 15, 1983), typescript, p. 1.

gion's need was great, and with President Few's leadership Duke met its responsibilities in this place, for it was with the South that Duke was appropriately and "immediately concerned," as Dr. Few expressed it. Today we pledge to continue meeting our responsibilities here, but we redefine the boundaries of Duke's immediate concerns. The world has grown close and increasingly dangerous. Chaotic conditions around the globe are no longer distant. We are in desperate need of responsible citizens for the world, and I believe that Duke University is uniquely positioned to meet that need.

There are many here who share this dream of Duke as an international university. It is not a recent hope, nor is it one that comes to us from strangers. It is a vision that has grown naturally with the people who built Duke University. This institution was blessed in the 1920s and '30s with brilliant and vigorous young scholars who brought Duke their international interests and found here a place that welcomed and cherished them. I am thinking now of scholars like Alan K. Manchester, who received his Ph.D. here in Latin American history in 1930—the tenth Ph.D. awarded at Duke; he became one of the nation's leading Brazilian scholars of his time. There was a climate on the Duke campus in the 1930s which looked toward our responsibility to the world at a time when America was officially and popularly committed to isolationism. Dr. Ruth Addoms, the first woman to hold professorial rank in our botany department, typified the high level of international activism among Duke faculty; for her role in British war relief, England awarded her the King's Medal for Service in the Cause of Freedom. During this period Duke proved to be extraordinarily receptive to world citizens who emigrated from Europe to escape the Nazi terror. Among them we should remember Fritz London, the brilliant German professor of chemical physics whose tragic early death deprived him of a Nobel prize.

Many of those who built this school in the 1930s were Rhodes scholars, and naturally they brought to Duke an international attitude. We might recall that one of these was Wilburt Davison, who came here from Johns Hopkins to build the Medical Center. After the Second World War Duke was one of six major American universities that led the way in bringing German students to study in this country. Later, in the 1950s, Duke's distinguished political scientist R. Taylor Cole presided over the birth and development of our Commonwealth Studies Center, and his active involvement with the developing countries of Africa in the 1960s brought to Duke a prescient voice of warning.

Our duty today is, I firmly believe, an international one, and I am preparing to take a number of steps to expand our influence and activity. I shall work with the provost to achieve our goal that every Duke student will be able to take one semester abroad. I plan to attend the next meeting of the Council of European Rectors, the standing conference of presidents of European universities. I shall there represent the institutions of the Association of American Universities (AAU) and shall join the effort to find our common boundaries of information, ideas, and human understanding with Eastern and Western Europe. And I hope that in similar ways we can reach out to the Third World. It is my hope that Duke will become even better known for its international programs. Indeed, Duke's history, resources, and outstanding faculty suggest to me that it has become our solemn obligation to serve the world community, just as it once was our duty to serve the South.

In 1910 President Few charged Trinity with a pressing duty: to educate for civic responsibility men and women who could lift the South's people out of poverty. In that charge to the college, we see how firmly this institution has been committed to the reality of its place and time, to the truly great needs of its community in the present as well as for the future. In reading that remarkable call for service to the real world, I cannot help thinking of John Adams' famous analysis of the duties assigned to himself and succeeding generations by their place and time in American history:

"I must study politics and war," he wrote to his beloved Abigail in 1780, "that my sons may have liberty to study mathematics and philosophy. My sons ought to study mathematics and philosophy, geography . . . navigation, commerce, and agriculture, in order to give their children a right to study painting, poetry, music. . . ."[7]

We are grateful that, as the South has prospered, so has Duke been enabled to go beyond its initial responsibilities. To the many duties subsumed in the word "teacher," Duke long ago began adding another. Today I would like to renew our commitment to those things which are the proper end of freedom, political stability, and economic prosperity—the things of the human spirit. At Duke our students are filling classes in art and art history, our excellent theaters and music building are burgeoning with activity, our still young Institute of the Arts has brought innumerable distinguished performers to this campus. These activities should be supported and expanded. For our students I would like Duke to offer a master's degree in fine arts. The performance concentration that such a degree makes possible would enrich the understanding of our students who study the fine arts and increase yet again the opportunities for arts performance and interpretation on this campus. For our larger community I would like to see an increased sharing of the arts; Durham and Duke should be sharing artists and sharing audiences. I would specifically like to see the American Dance Festival broaden its base, becoming part of an active and vital arts complex in downtown Durham.

I sincerely believe that it would be wrong for a university with our resources, our scope and reputation, to do nothing—or nothing significant—to support the visual and performing arts. They are the most vulnerable, the most fragile of activities in our

7. John Adams to Abigail Adams, 12 May 1780, in *The Book of Abigail and John: Selected Letters of the Adams Family 1762–1784*, ed. L. H. Butterfield, et al. (Cambridge: Harvard University Press, 1975), p. 260. Spelling and capitalization have been modernized.

society. When funding is scarce they are the first to go. When audiences are lacking they wither. When society is unsympathetic and uncomprehending the arts die. As a university we have many duties, among them to seek the truth in all knowledge, new and old, and to seek the wisdom. I doubt that we can perform this duty without the presence of beauty, imagination, and love. Our fifth president, Douglas Knight, once instructed us in this matter. "A great mind," he said, "is monstrous, after all, if it is wedded to a petty heart."[8]

To achieve wisdom, the human spirit must be spoken to in the special languages of the arts.

With color and line, the artist makes visible a religious truth. In space and air the dancer leaps—and momentarily explains hope.

Somewhere a playwright and a troupe of actors recall the meaning of ancient tragedy. From the Soviet Union a great composer smuggles out a message about human freedom—and a symphony orchestra breaks the code.

The arts enlarge our vision, recreate our humanity, and instruct our hearts. They express what we otherwise cannot say.

We need them.

One lifetime ago, Trinity College marked a special beginning here in Durham. A star danced that year as well. I would like to take the return of Halley's comet in 1910 and now in 1985 as a sign—for we do believe in signs, somehow, in portents and rituals. Our ceremonies this afternoon are evidence of that.

Halley's comet has returned to our heavens, and I want to take it as a sign for the new hopes of this university. I do not say that this star dances for me, but rather for our good beginnings that require celebration and joy and for our inexpressible hopes that require a sign.

8. Douglas M. Knight, President-Elect (Duke University), *Founder's Day Address, Duke University: The Stones of the House* (Durham, N.C.: Duke University, Dec. 10, 1962), p. 18.

Of Cultures and Anarchy

By the spring of 1988 the composition of the Duke Board of Trustees was much changed from the days when I had served as chancellor for President Terry Sanford. Many more members brought backgrounds as corporate CEO's, and nearly half had been seated since my becoming president on July 1, 1985. Thus, ours was a rather young board in terms of experience with leading Duke and generally in terms of experience with higher education. Of course, all new trustees participated in orientation sessions conducted by university officers, faculty, and our board chair. In these sessions we covered such topics as academics, the Medical Center, budget and financial operations, and the role and responsibilities of trustees. I usually spoke on the teaching, research, and service missions of the university, its history and general organizational structure, and some of the particular issues and tensions facing us. Finally, I always summarized our expectations of trusteeship as work, wealth, and wisdom—opening doors for us and networking, contributing tangible support to the university, and sharing their advice through regular attendance at meetings and conscientious committee service.

But a day or so of orientation and a year or two of quarterly meetings are not enough for even the brightest and most successful of people to adapt a lifetime of profit-and-loss thinking to the world of the university. Our trustees were struggling to learn a new template for measuring and guiding corporate operations. They were ready and eager to contribute their expertise to Duke, but the difference between their roles as directors on corporate boards and as trustees of a research university was not yet clear to them, much less second nature as it was to us.

At the time I undertook the comparisons in the following speech, we were faced with many areas of concern common to our peer institutions: the need to raise revenue by raising tuition while simultaneously increasing financial aid to insure a diverse student body; a backlog of deferred maintenance; critical needs for new academic space; and the rapidly escalating costs of scientific research and teaching, especially the expense of equipping university laboratories with state-of-the-art technology. In addition, at Duke we were committed to increasing faculty salaries as part of our continuing rise into the top tier of research universities, and we were undertaking long-range planning for use of our land resources. While the October 1987 downturn in the stock market had hurt the market value of many college and university endowments, thanks to Senior Vice President Eugene McDonald's prudent oversight of our endowment, Duke was not seriously affected. Nonetheless, we were in the midst of a major capital campaign to increase an endowment that was significantly smaller than the endowments of universities with which we were competing. The faculty and I were involved in the once-in-a-decade self-study required for reaccreditation by the Southern Association of Colleges and Schools, and our Academic Council's Task Force on University Governance had just issued its interim report, calling for a more open approach to budgeting and resource allocation on the part of the administration and stronger guidelines for faculty involvement in institutional decision making. Clearly, the time was ripe for some additional trustee education.

ADDRESS TO THE BOARD OF TRUSTEES OF DUKE UNIVERSITY MAY 6, 1988

This morning we shall be discussing plans—plans that have emerged as the result of our several years of planning effort. We bring these plans to you for comment, to guide us as we create priorities for your approval at future meetings. Though many of you are familiar with differences between corporate and academic planning, I thought it would be useful if I introduced our discussions by highlighting the special features which differentiate a university such as Duke from a corporation.

I would like to begin by noting a planning effort at Duke that went awry and that, in its comical awryness, illustrates some of the important qualities of the "house of intellect" that I will share with you today.

It all began innocently enough in the early spring of 1966. President Douglas Knight, seeking a way to raise university salaries across the board, hit upon the idea of hiring corporate management consultants to look into the possibilities for more efficient use of personnel in the nonacademic sectors of the university. Perhaps savings could be realized, he conjectured, through university-wide planning efforts in housekeeping, grounds, and maintenance. Thus, a personnel committee was convened, consultants submitted their proposals, and so it was that the Alexander Proudfoot Company of One North La Salle Street, Chicago, Illinois, was engaged to carry out something called—ominously enough—Proudfoot Scheduling Installations.[1]

The Proudfoot people descended upon the hospital and the campus, created elaborate and impressive flow charts, and near the end of July the fatal misstep was taken: they recommended that their efficiency analysis be extended to support services in the academic areas of the university. The first signs of real trouble, however, emanated from the laundry, where the Proudfeet had installed their scheduling system during the summer without taking into account the change in workloads when students returned to

1. Correspondence and memoranda related to the Proudfoot Scheduling Installations, March 31, 1966–May 12, 1967, records of the Office of the President—Douglas M. Knight, Duke University Archives.

school for the fall semester. When confronted with complaints, the Proudfoot representative accused the housekeeping supervisors of "sabotage."

Meanwhile, the Proudfooters fanned out over the Duke campus. In response to expressions of concern from the Divinity School came scarcely veiled charges that Divinity had "no desire to operate more economically." To further illuminate the obstructive behavior of Divinity, it was pointed out that Roger Marshall, director of alumni and loyalty, had presented the Proudfoot system in "the most enthusiastic and positive approach we've experienced here at Duke." Apparently Roger, in his infinite and practical wisdom, had simply assured his staff that nobody was going to be fired.

If, in the opinion of Proudfoot, the Divinity School was obstinate and uninterested in economical operation, then the Law School must have been put down for criminal intent. From the Office of the Dean came a three-page memo of outrage, stating that the "Scheduling Installations" were turning the Law School into a "sweat shop." "We simply cannot live with these procedures . . . without severely damaging our educational program," Dean F. Hodge O'Neal wrote. "Incidentally," he continued, "from the conversations I have had with people in other departments, it is apparent that there is a smouldering but intense resentment to the imposition of [the Proudfoot] procedures among administrators and faculty. . . ."

This was in the spring of 1967, one year after the Proudfoot plan had been solicited. By now smoulderings in the library, which had been noted the previous fall, had burst into flame. "Morale of the once happy and dedicated staff could scarcely be lower," wrote University Librarian Ben Powell. "The presence of observers and stopwatches . . . is resented." Ben concluded that the failure of the Proudfoot associates lay "in their basic assumption which precludes their ever taking into account the values and ends which are the [Research] Library's reason for being."

An alarmed Faculty Library Council met in special session to declare the Proudfoot system unworkable, and one month later faculty and library staff confronted the Proudfoot associates for the last time, here in the board room. In a heated exchange Ben Powell asserted that the Proudfoot observers, "[can't] recognize work when it is performed before them," and after a forty-minute defense and subsequent cross-examination during which the Proudfoot representative denied that the system was nothing more than a time and motion study, the fate of the Proudfoot Scheduling Installations at Duke University was sealed: when asked by a professor if the Proudfoot philosophy "could be applied to the work of the faculty," the naive consultant replied in the affirmative.

In retrospect the engagement of the Proudfoot consultants seems ludicrously wrongheaded; after all, even their stationery advertised misunderstanding, for it boasted "operating effectiveness" for "manufacturing, product costing, maintenance, distribution and warehousing." This clash of cultures, worthy of a Henry James novel, is perhaps exaggerated, but exaggerated illustrations are useful: like good jokes they remind us of certain fundamental facts about human nature or, in this case, the fundamental facts about universities and faculties and the peculiarly inefficient nature of their enterprise.

In comparing universities to corporations, the legendary president of the University of California, Clark Kerr, once observed that academic institutions are concerned with "inputs, not outputs . . . there is no quarterly test of profit or loss." One of our difficulties in measuring outputs, profits, and losses is our time frame: we operate most effectively in a generational mode. Watching for the return on human capital is rather like waiting to count the accretion of tree rings in a particularly valuable wood. One's great-grandchildren will know best the results of one's choices in soil and cultivation.

If pressed, we might construct as our profit side of the sheet an honor role of alumni, respected for their humanitarian achievements, discoveries of knowledge, and leadership and responsibility in society at large. But what of the loss side of the ledger? How to count human capital wasted—the students who came to Duke but were lost? the students who never came to Duke and were lost for want of scholarship funds or encouragement or of explanation for the possibilities of a particular life in our place and time?

Well, these are visionary matters in which we deal, not amenable to ledgers and the ordinary accounting methods of good stewardship. But it is the specific demands of accountable stewardship that bring us into areas of paradox and that most concern us in our roles as administrators and leaders of Duke. A 1973 Carnegie report, describing the university as an organization, in one section develops an analogy of the university with the corporation. Inevitably its author comes banging up against the knotty problem of students, as so many of us do. You see, it is difficult to place them in the corporate paradigm, for students, on the one hand, arrive on campus as the consumers of our product; a few years later, however, they leave the campus, having become the product.[2]

Faculty also hold a somewhat paradoxical position in that, while they draw salaries from the university, they are not really employees in the usual sense. For example, once faculty are hired and granted tenure, they cannot be fired except under the most extraordinary circumstances. They have virtually a lifetime contract. Thus, the relationship between the faculty and the university is less like corporate employment than it is like a marriage.

2. Ralph M. Besse, "A Comparison of the University with the Corporation," in *The University as an Organization: A Report for the Carnegie Commission on Higher Education*, ed. James A. Perkins (New York: Carnegie Foundation for the Advancement of Teaching [McGraw Hill Book Co.], 1973), p. 120.

Let us continue the comparison. Consider the matter of promotion to an administrative position. The chairmanship of an academic department is less a promotion than it is a personal sacrifice. Phil Stewart and Al Kornberg are with us today—past and current chairs of their respective departments. They undertook these positions as a matter of service, even devotion to their responsibilities as professors. The administrative leadership role does not enhance academic careers, it interrupts them by taking scholars away from their pursuit of scholarship. And when, after facing difficult decisions at the departmental level, the academic administrator steps down, he or she sometimes finds as reward a residue of personal animus among colleagues, one of whom may be responsible for setting the former chair's salary in subsequent years. Thus, while the role of administrator represents advancement in the corporate world, such is not necessarily the case among academics.

I believe it was the poet Robert Frost who once pointed out that the universities belong to the scholars.[3] And so they do, for it is the scholars who carry out the primary mission of the university, and in ways quite different from those of a corporate employee. The best and most creative academic talent is drawn to a university such as Duke for the sake of stimulation and interaction with like-gifted colleagues; for the quality of students, both graduate and undergraduate; for the academic facilities, such as laboratories and research libraries; but most of all, for intellectual freedom. The Duke professoriate are an extraordinarily gifted group of free thinking, freewheeling, disruptive spirits who have chosen to be here precisely because this is not a corporation; here the incentives are different, the measures of performance are different,

3. Robert Frost, audiotape of a speech given March 3, 1961, in Memorial Hall at the University of North Carolina, North Carolina Collection, Wilson Library, the University of North Carolina at Chapel Hill.

perhaps most notably, the workstyles, time frames, expectations, and goals are different. And it follows that effective leadership of such an organization of individuals would be very different from effective leadership of a corporation. As a former president of Indiana University succinctly puts it, "The house of intellect is by nature averse to orders."[4]

Therefore, as leader of this university and a member of its faculty, my role in its broadest sense is to serve, to facilitate, and to support the efforts of our faculty within the university's mission of teaching, research, and service to society. In reflecting on this kind of leadership, we recall the nature of a list of ideal attributes prepared by our president emeritus, Terry Sanford, at the request of Duke's presidential search committee. Only a handful of the characteristics Terry named might be considered qualities directly applicable to the role of CEO of a major corporation. Rather, the majority of the sought-after qualities—qualities such as tolerance, compassion, and the unwillingness to allow injustice—tend toward the moral. Terry's ideal university president possesses knowledge and qualities of the mind and spirit which indicate that he or she understands the university's main activity—the transmittal and discovery of knowledge—and the humane nature of its mission of service.

Thus, it is essential that faculty at a university such as Duke have a firm sense of moral leadership at the helm, that is, confidence that the leader of the university is seeking to do the right thing in support of the agreed-upon mission of the institution and the values for which it stands. Such a confidence is absolutely essential for consensus, which is the accepted and indeed only workable mode of decision making at a university. And by consensus here, I do not mean a matter of simple majority opinion,

4. Herman B Wells, *Being Lucky: Reminiscences and Reflections* (Bloomington: Indiana University Press, 1980), p. 119.

though that is certainly one of the meanings of the word. Rather, I mean consent based on belief in the good-faith motivations of all concerned.

But what of the choices and decisions that must be made by the president and board of trustees in the business operations of a complex institution such as Duke? What of the "inevitable pain and controversy"—as Gene [Eugene McDonald] reminded us last February—that are attendant upon putting to work finite resources in support of infinite hopes and dreams? We have at Duke an organizational structure that encourages departments, divisions, and schools to practice a certain amount of autonomy. In this way, and by means of formulas, incentives are provided to each academic unit to operate both so as to effect savings and to seek additional outside funding, while at the same time recognizing an overarching allegiance to the university as a whole.

Sometimes that recognition does not come happily, as cherished plans are delayed, temporarily shelved, or in some instances dropped entirely because of the university's needs as one balanced institution. At these times it is imperative that the president do everything possible to ensure that all concerned have been involved, that all interests have been fairly heard and considered. Our faculty do not expect to agree with every decision taken in the administering of such a large and complicated entity as this university; they do expect that decisions will be reached openly, judiciously, and in good faith with the stated missions and goals of the institution. Only through such a process can consensus be granted, and only by consensus can this institution be effectively guided.

The best way to build consensus is through a planning process that takes into account both the long life of the institution and the immediate concerns of all our constituencies. Not only does long-term planning enable us to identify, conserve, and deploy our resources most effectively for future needs and growth, but it also fosters the openness and involvement and creates the broad understanding and the time that consensus requires. Consensus building takes time. It is difficult to achieve under crisis management conditions.

So today we continue that process of consensus building, asking you for your thoughts on our aspirations and our dreams for this great university.

Girls and Women in Sports

February 4, 1989, was the third time our nation and our state celebrated Girls and Women in Sports Day, proclaimed in Washington by the White House and in North Carolina by Governor Jim Martin "to call attention to the positive influence that sports participation has on women's lives." One of the ways to do that was to honor women and girls who had shown outstanding achievement in sports at an event organized by North Carolina Amateur Sports. In 1987 Chancellor Chris Fordham of the University of North Carolina had welcomed the celebration to Chapel Hill, and the following year participants gathered in Raleigh at North Carolina State University, where they were greeted by Chancellor Bruce Poulton. When our turn came at Duke, I was delighted to learn that the keynote speaker would be a Duke alumna, Olympic swimmer Nancy Hogshead, who had returned from Los Angeles in the summer of 1984 with four medals—three gold and one silver—ready to take up where she had left off at Duke, i.e., her junior year. In addition, two Duke women were among the special honorees: Assistant Athletic Director Lorraine Woodyard and the head coach of our nationally ranked women's tennis team, Jane Preyer.

Because I knew the occasion would be especially meaningful for students and teachers across the state and that the presence of celebrity Nancy Hogshead would guarantee press coverage, I contacted a number of Duke coaches to ask their advice about my "brief welcoming remarks." In the few minutes allotted to me, what issues should I raise? what could I say that might be of help? I was surprised by the intensity and unanimity with which the answer came back: a university president taking a public stand with a strong personal message of support and respect for women's sports would mean a great deal to all women involved in intercollegiate athletics. I realized then that the necessity for most NCAA presidents to monitor continuously the big revenue sports for rules violations and abuses had led us as a group to speak out less often and less publicly than we should have about the importance, the achievements, and the potential of our women's programs, a potential that Title IX had ironically undermined in one significant way.

ADDRESS TO THE PARTICIPANTS NORTH CAROLINA GIRLS AND WOMEN IN SPORTS DAY FEBRUARY 4, 1989

Let me begin by saying how pleased I am to be welcoming you to Duke University for this celebration of girls and women in sports. My first reaction to the letter of invitation from North Carolina Coordinator Winkie La Force was, "Good! We need to celebrate and recognize girls and women in sports." Frankly, ours is a society that has not offered equal support and encouragement to female participation in sports, to gifted female athletes, nor to women who wish to pursue sports-related careers. In the past fifteen years or so, our attitudes and behavior as a society have been changing, but not enough. According to one woman prominent in intercollegiate sports—Donna Lopiano of Texas—we are maybe halfway to where we ought to be in supporting women who want to compete,[1] and I would guess that we are probably only halfway to where we ought to be in encouraging and providing opportunities for all women to consider sports as vital a part of their development and continuing health as do men.

1. Donna Lopiano, Women's Athletic Director, University of Texas, Austin, telephone interview with Leslie Banner, February 1, 1989.

It says a great deal, I think, that Governor Martin has not proclaimed a North Carolina Boys and Men in Sports Day. Every day in our culture is Boys and Men in Sports Day. We take it for granted that the males of our society should develop the skills and share in the benefits of sports. But we have not taken it for granted that our girls and women should also share in these benefits equally. My thoughts about these benefits—and my concerns—arise from numerous conversations with our coaches here at Duke and with coaches at other universities and from three personal points of view: as a physician, as a psychiatrist, and as the leader of an educational institution that influences thousands of young lives.

Early in my training as an M.D., I became aware of how important it is for people to truly inhabit their own bodies, that is, to cultivate a sense of physical awareness that promotes good health. We might consider taking proper care of our bodies as a kind of physical morality that requires us to treat ourselves with respect. Proper nutrition, medical care, and disciplined movement are all part of respecting our physical selves. And sports might be described as the most pleasurable tool for living according to a high standard of physical morality. Isn't it extraordinary that only relatively recently has our society embraced the concept that women as much as men need strong, skilled, reliable bodies? Participation in sports is the best way to teach girls as well as boys to ensure those bodies.

As a psychiatrist I have become especially sensitized to the effect that sports can have in developing psychological resources in young people. Every one of you here today can cite, I am sure, the list of character traits I have in mind—traits such as self-discipline, self-confidence, the sense of fair play, cooperativeness, and perhaps most important as women emerge from a male-dominated society, the sense of mastery that is developed in the skilled athlete. These traits are most important in the development of leadership skills: sports participation offers practice in group motivation, conflict resolution, goal-directed behavior, personal initiative, and team bonding—skills that help create leaders for every profession. And it is this question of leadership training that brings me to my third point of view and my greatest concern as an educator.

Providing effective, positive role models is one of the most important ways that higher education can help young people choose their life's work and attain their full majority as effective citizens. Yet, in regard to sports-related careers for women, higher education has fallen down on the job. Since the implementation of Title IX, opportunities for women to participate in intercollegiate sports have increased dramatically, but, as the women's athletic director at the University of Minnesota, Chris Voelz, recently pointed out, the number of women in collegiate sports leadership positions has declined drastically.[2] According to a national study of all NCAA institutions that offer intercollegiate athletic programs for women, in 1972 over 90 percent of women's teams were coached by women. Today, despite the fact that the number of sports offered for women has increased, the percentage of female coaches has dropped to 48 percent. In athletic administration the numbers are even worse: in 1972 90 percent of women's programs were directed by women. Today only 16 percent are being run by female athletic directors.[3] Although I have not seen complete state-by-state data on sports in our secondary schools, the partial data available suggest strongly that since 1972 the percentage of girls' sports coached by women at the high school level has seen a similar sharp decline.[4]

2. Chris Voelz, Women's Athletic Director, University of Minnesota, Minneapolis, Minnesota, telephone interview with Leslie Banner, February 1, 1989.

3. R. Vivian Acosta and Linda Jean Carpenter, "Women in Intercollegiate Sport: *A Longitudinal Study—Eleven-Year Update 1977–1988*," Department of Physical Education, Brooklyn College, Brooklyn, New York.

4. Carolyn A. Cody, "Employment Trends and Opportunities for Women in Sport Leadership Positions," ERIC document, April 1985, p. 5.

The opening up of opportunities for women to participate in sports has been very important and we have made much progress, but young women who pursue sports intensively and who have the genuine desire to share the benefits of sports with others in a variety of ways deserve to have open to them the same career ladder that is open to men—from athlete to high school or college coach; from coach to athletic director; from athlete or sports enthusiast to official, athletic trainer, or sports information director. Yet today, paradoxically, these occupations remain for the most part only theoretically open to women. To quote from an interesting unpublished study of employment data on women in sports, the opportunities to compete that were gained through the federal mandate of Title IX "have diverted our attention from who is providing leadership for competitive young females. We have failed to notice who was at the bench, on the sidelines, in the training room, the board room, the press box and [at] the officials table."[5]

The reasons for this failure are varied, most deriving from the fact that in a time of great social change all things cannot be accomplished at once. The years of less funding and fewer opportunities in women's sports meant that the field of competitive experience was deeper among men when Title IX was implemented; and the problem of a lack of female leadership became self-perpetuating. Today we must find and nurture the competitive young women who can and should be filling their share of the leadership positions in sports, and all leaders of collegiate sports programs need to be mindful of and to cherish the earlier, pre-Title IX tradition of women's sports in higher education—the tradition of preserving and protecting our commitment to the true student athlete. Or, in the blunt words of Texan Donna Lopiano, "Graduation has *never* been an issue with women athletes."

5. Cody, p. 12.

And, I might add, let us make sure that it never will be.

For me these days, the overriding concerns about girls and women in sports are the issues of athletic excellence in the context of a college education and the vision of unlimited opportunity for every young woman to look forward to doing the meaningful work of her choice. I applaud all of you here today for gathering to talk about and to celebrate women in sports at every age and level and in every context. It is vitally important to raise the awareness of our society to the imbalance in the status of women in athletics, to the achievements of women in sports, and to the potential that sports offer all women to discover for themselves a fuller citizenship and a higher quality of life.

Enjoy your time together here today. My warmest congratulations to your special honorees.

3

SPEAKING OF STUDENTS

How to Become a Genius

From the mid-1970s onward, America's college students as a group appeared to have lost the idealism that had characterized the sixties, when young people vigorously protested social injustices and entered the helping professions and the Peace Corps in great numbers. Thus, when the Duke presidency increased my involvement with our undergraduate colleges (Trinity College of Arts and Sciences and the School of Engineering), I was pleasantly surprised to find that a spirit of social activism was once again on the rise among our students. I got to know them—and their concerns—through a number of avenues, both formal and informal: in my undergraduate seminars in psychobiology, where I taught seniors in the fall semester and first-year students in the spring; during open office hours several mornings a week, when individual students came to me for personal advice or for help with special projects that fell outside the established student organizations; through invited participation in student-initiated events such as Earth Day or the Julian Abele Banquet;[1] *as colleagues in university governance, either as student government officers or student representatives on innumerable*

1. Julian Abele (1881–1950), a distinguished Philadelphia architect whose work included Harvard's Widener Library and the Philadelphia Museum of Art, is now recognized as the designer of most of Duke's Neo-Gothic West Campus. Abele, who was a member of the Horace Trumbauer firm, never saw the Duke campus, and it is unclear whether Duke officials of the time realized that he was black.

Duke University committees, task forces, and advisory groups; and, yes, as protesters, who circulated petitions for day care at Duke and built shanties to urge us to divest the university's portfolio of stock in companies doing business in South Africa. As president, I am happy to say, I learned a lot about our students, and one of the things I learned most about was their fervent commitment to voluntarism and their determination to act according to the dictates of conscience.

Graduation at Duke did not include any extensive remarks by the president during the commencement ceremonies; instead, each year the senior class looked forward to being addressed by someone notable in the wider world and a ceremony that lasted little more than an hour during a usually hot and humid time of year. In the fall, therefore, it became my custom to sponsor a reception for the senior class where I could offer parting advice. This timing permitted me one last pitch for the value of their liberal arts education while they still had a semester left for it and gave me a chance not only to applaud their achievements as campus citizens, but also to encourage them to continue their commitment to good citizenship as they had practiced it at Duke.

ADDRESS TO THE SENIOR CLASS
DUKE UNIVERSITY
OCTOBER 5, 1988

It is my pleasure at this time to announce the name of the 1989 commencement speaker. As you know, the commencement committee is composed of representatives from our student body, faculty, and administration who nominate a person of character and distinction to speak to our graduating classes on this high occasion in the life of the university. While our commencement speakers come from a variety of backgrounds, they share the characteristics of having something substantive to say and of knowing how to say it well. I can think of no better succinct description of the committee's choice for 1989, a man who is internationally recognized as one of a very rare breed: a scientist highly respected within his own discipline who writes regularly about science for nonscientists.

Currently at the center of an ongoing and quite serious scientific controversy about expanded evolutionary theory, your speaker has nonetheless written a series of books that have won for him unabashed literary accolades: the National Magazine Award for his monthly column in *Natural History* magazine, the 1981 American Book Award for *The Panda's Thumb*, the 1982 National Book Critics Circle Award for *The Mismeasure of Man*, the 1983 Phi Beta Kappa Book Award for *Hen's Teeth and Horse's Toes*, the 1987 American Academy and Institute of Arts and Letters Award for the "quality of [his] prose style." The list of awards and recognitions is lengthy and comes from admirers as far afield as the Zoological Society of London and *Rolling Stone* magazine, which honored him with an interview last year and dubbed him the "scourge of creationists."[2]

I am speaking, of course, of the living answer to that perennial question, can a *real* scientist serve on the advisory boards of NOVA and the Children's Television Workshop and still get respect? Yes, he can, if his name is Professor Stephen Jay Gould. I am delighted to be able to tell you that this eminent paleontologist, geologist, biologist, zoologist, and writer has accepted Duke University's invitation to join us for our 1989 commencement.

When we march together next May—you and I who came in together as freshmen, freshman students and a freshman president—there should be 1,294 of you, giving the class of '89 a graduation rate of more than 90 percent. Most of you indicate plans for the future similar to those of last year's seniors. About 41 percent will go on to further study next fall, either in graduate or professional schools. This means that 59 percent will travel

2. John Tierney, "Stephen Jay Gould: The *Rolling Stone* Interview," *Rolling Stone*, January 15, 1987, 38.

or seek employment after graduation. Approximately 150 of you have applied to medical school and we expect that 95 percent will be accepted. Three hundred and thirty-one members of your class hope to go on to law school, and based on last year's acceptance rate, virtually all will be admitted. The one dramatic difference in future plans between your class and last year's is the increase in the number applying to business schools: more than twice as many members of the class of '89—50 of you—plan to seek M.B.A.'s immediately rather than choosing to work a year or two first.

This brings me to the heart of my talk with you today. The president's address to the senior class at Duke University has become a tradition, and certain topics in my addresses to the senior class have themselves become traditional: announcing the commencement speaker; collecting and analyzing our most recent statistical data in order to profile your class; and offering you some advice for the future, which is, after all, the prerogative of a commencement speaker and I am rather in the position of being the precommencement speaker, the warm-up act, if you will, for next spring. So I take it as part of my bona fide mission this afternoon to give you advice.

Now, there are those among the student body each year—and they are a minority, I believe, but nonetheless a vocal minority—who imply that giving advice on a regular basis is not all that difficult and therefore such speeches of advice should always be fresh and entirely new. Well, I would like to say this: in my experience—especially since becoming a university president—there just isn't that much good advice going around. And when your job requires that you traffic in eternal verities on a regular basis, the problem is obviously considerably compounded. However, nobody said that being president of Duke was going to be easy, so today I am prepared to offer you a compromise: good, *old* advice in a new speech. I have entitled this speech "How to Become a Genius," and I guarantee that no one except my kids and

1. If it rained the inauguration was to be held in Duke Chapel, but happily September 28, 1985 was a clear 73 degrees and an omen—the university and I were thereafter blessed with eight sunny commencements. Notable on the platform are two North Carolina governors (second and third from my left): Terry Sanford and James G. Martin. Behind us, the Duke University Symphony and Wind Symphony and the chapel. (photo by Jim Wallace)

2. In the fall of 1985, as concern about apartheid intensified on campus, I appointed a student-faculty-trustee committee to study the social implications of Duke's investments in South Africa. In November, a student referendum showed that 57 percent of those who voted favored divestment, and the following February the Duke student government adopted a resolution calling for complete divestment. On May 6, 1986, as recommended by the committee, our board of trustees voted to divest. (photo by Les Todd)

3. We were concerned that evangelist Billy Graham, exhausted from a crusade behind the Iron Curtain, might not be able to preach in Duke Chapel on November 17, 1985 as part of the chapel's fiftieth anniversary celebration. But his vigor and obvious good health radiated from the pulpit as he preached a spellbinding sermon on the Twenty-third Psalm. It was a privilege to meet with him informally in Reverend Will Willimon's office before the service. (photo by Jim Wallace)

4. On Sunday, January 19, 1986, Bishop Desmond Tutu's small chartered plane was late and the crowd awaiting him in Duke Chapel sang hymn after hymn until suddenly, in a truly electrifying moment, the doors of the chapel flew open and the bishop entered. Later, after his stirring message of faith in God against the evils of apartheid, Bishop Tutu and I talked during a reception in the basement of the Divinity School. (photo by Les Todd)

5. Ted Koppel, host of *ABC News Nightline* and, on May 10, 1987, the proud father of an eager-to-graduate Duke senior, received a rare standing ovation at commencement after reminding his audience, "What Moses brought down from Mt. Sinai were not the Ten Suggestions." Here, we posed with two of his fellow honorees, philanthropist R. David Thomas, the founder of Wendy's, and Dr. Mary L. Good, president of the American Chemical Society, the world's largest scientific organization, and, the following year, chair of the National Science Board. (photo by Jim Wallace)

6. We sent the basketball team out to greet President Ronald Reagan when his helicopter set down on our lacrosse field in the early afternoon of February 8, 1988. The president was attending a conference on substance abuse in the workplace sponsored by Governor Jim Martin and Duke University. I joined the panel in Cameron Indoor Stadium and made President Reagan an honorary Blue Devil. (photo by Les Todd)

7. Each year following my welcoming address to the entering class, my wife Brenda and I looked forward to encountering the excitement of the new students and their parents at an outdoor reception held variously on East or West Campus. Brenda, a graduate of the Columbia University School of Nursing, proved to be a tireless supporter of Duke as she oversaw the operations of the president's Guest House and hosted or attended innumerable "special events" on behalf of the university. (photo by Les Todd)

8. On August 28, 1988, in a very hot Cameron Indoor Stadium, orientation became a community-wide event as over 6,500 Duke students, employees, and Durham citizens gathered to hear the rousing words of the Reverend Jesse L. Jackson. (photo by Les Todd)

9. Duke parent and *NBC Nightly News* anchor Tom Brokaw generously stepped in after the tragic death of his friend and our scheduled speaker for Commencement 1990, baseball commissioner Bart Giamatti. Tom achieved the impossible—near silence among the graduates in Wallace Wade as he challenged them to use their Duke educations "as a national resource." (photo by Jim Wallace)

10. Brenda's service as president of the Durham Day Care Council had first heightened my awareness of the need at Duke. When our students joined employees in enthusiastic endorsement of the cause, I appointed a university task force on child care which began work in November of 1988. The Children's Campus, Duke University's child care center, opened on August 22, 1990. (photo by Ron Ferrell)

11. At our 1992 commencement I presented a doctor of humane letters to Marian Wright Edelman, founder of the Children's Defense Fund and our speaker. She urged Duke graduates to ask themselves, "How can I lose myself in service to others?" (photo by Jim Wallace)

12. Bobby Hurley's was the seventh basketball jersey to be retired at Duke (February 28, 1993) and my fifth such ceremony while president. I always enjoyed the excitement of these occasions, especially as anything I had to say was always drowned out by the cheering fans! (photo by Ron Ferrell)

13. Mickey Krzyzewski's involvement and support have been essential elements in the Blue Devils' success story, while Mike, through his willingness to speak to groups of donors — or potential donors — across the country, has benefited the university above and beyond the sphere of coaching. In fact, as a speaker at Duke alumni events, Mike was in greater demand than the president. (photo by Jim Wallace)

14. My "sign-up" lunches with students (under the auspices of the Duke University Union) in the Oak Room acquainted me with the big issues of the day among a cross-section of our students and allowed me to probe for special issues of concern or areas for praise. I frequently asked the group if anyone had an outstanding teacher that semester and followed up with basketball tickets for the professor named. (photo by Les Todd)

15. The Reverend Will Willimon, appointed minister to the university in 1984, has had great impact on campus life, challenging the Duke community well beyond his chapel pulpit. His inspirational baccalaureate sermons, thoughtfully referenced to our seniors' Duke experiences and tempered by Will's famous sense of humor, became an eagerly awaited graduation tradition. (photo by Jim Wallace)

16. Stepping down from the presidency allowed me to resume teaching the senior seminar I had given up at the trustees' request. As difficult as it is for a university president to find the time, continuing in the classroom with at least one course (as I did manage to insist on) provides an invaluable venue for learning current student thinking, for staying in touch with the faculty point of view, and for refreshing one's sense of vocation. (photo by Jim Wallace)

my cocker spaniel has ever heard it before. In it, I give you three major pieces of advice, and because good advice is not only hard to come by but even harder to follow, I have obligingly summarized my remarks as three basic rules to follow for becoming a genius at life: (1) learn irrelevant things, (2) find out what's wrong, and (3) welcome the hard times.

Let's start with one: learn irrelevant things. Stephen Jay Gould is an outstanding and pertinent example of why we need to know as much as we can about as many things as we can possibly find a way to explore. Professor Gould, the recipient in 1981 of one of the five-year MacArthur Foundation Prize Fellowships—the so-called "genius awards"—is known for the connections he makes between scientific disciplines, for seeing relationships among things, for identifying patterns that have eluded other researchers. Gould himself has said that "If genius has any common denominator, I would propose breadth of interest and the ability to construct fruitful analogies between fields."[3]

"Breadth of interest"—the willingness to be curious about everything you encounter, the courage to release energy down paths whose direction you cannot predict or control. No matter what your plans are for the future, this is a habit of mind that will serve you well. It is characteristic of the brilliant entrepreneurial mind in business that sees an opportunity where others don't even see a need, of the political mind that organizes a team of good people to solve a problem before other people recognize the problem exists, of the scientific mind that breaks another of life's codes, of the artistic mind that creates a new description of the human drama. Breadth of interest is one of the chief identifying traits of the best teachers, the best leaders, the best mothers and fathers, the best psychiatrists.

"The ability to construct fruitful analogies between fields"—

3. Stephen Jay Gould, "Darwin's Middle Road," in *The Panda's Thumb* (New York: W. W. Norton & Co., Inc., 1982), p. 66.

irrelevant things lead to breakthroughs. The discoveries that will occur in your lifetime will probably be made at the interface between existing disciplines: the linkage of music and computer science, of immunology and neurology, of mechanical engineering and biology. Our faculty have made significant careers at the interface—people like Stephen Wainwright [zoology] or Bruce Payne [public policy studies] or Theo Pilkington [biomedical engineering]. Try to tie your area of strength to another, perhaps seemingly irrelevant area that sparks your interest, and look at the interface—there you will find the greatest opportunity to contribute.

Life has taught me that nothing you learn is ever wasted; it's what you don't know that can hurt you. So my message to you is this: when you arrange your spring schedule, look at the offerings in some of the departments and programs that are not familiar to you. If you don't see the immediate relevance of a particular course to your future plans, then take that course! Apparent *ir*relevance is probably the best criterion of all, and recognizing its importance is the first step in becoming a genius.

This brings us to rule number 2: find out what's wrong. For the past three years at Duke, you have explored issues of moral responsibility, trying to determine what your values are. You have listened to speakers ranging from Billy Graham to Adolfo Calero, from Robert Bork to Ralph Nader. You have heard Robert McNamara and Maki Mandela, Elie Wiesel and Abbie Hoffman, Ronald Reagan, Jesse Jackson, and Bishop Tutu. You have tried to find out what is wrong in the world and what you can do to make it right. And in that cause you have rallied against apartheid and for divestment, you have supported increasing black faculty, and you have taken back the night and invented the stop card.[4] You

4. On November 19, 1987, the Coalition for a Women's Center sponsored Duke's first Take Back the Night march, a student-led protest of violence against women that has become an annual event at Duke. In the spring of 1987 Duke

have noted discrimination in the classroom and you are helping to formulate policies to address it. You have served the university as its conscience, focusing the attention of the administration on the need to invest in low-income housing in our community. You have pressed for the creation of a women's center and for the provision of child care for those who work and study here. You have endorsed the protection of our forest as an irreplaceable asset, a precious heirloom. You have pressed us to repair our classrooms and dormitories, and you have convinced us to address our problem with overcrowding through the construction of a new dormitory. When you leave this university, it will be a better institution because of your efforts.

You have also supported the efforts of your fellow Duke students who are athletes, showing your pride in them for maintaining high ethical standards of sportsmanship as well as standards of excellence in competition. And even when you cheered for our championship teams, you remembered to say, we're proud of you for winning *and* for graduating. You will always remember the death of Len Bias,[5] and you will be able to say that during a time of national scandal in college athletics, your university was recognized as a national model for honest yet competitive sports. In years ahead, when you hear disappointing stories such as those

---

Public Safety began using the "stop card," which had been created by a committee of students and public safety officers in response to student concerns about identification checks on the Duke campus which seemed to affect black students disproportionately. When an officer stopped a student and asked to see Duke identification, the student received in return a card listing the officer's name, date and time of the stop, and phone numbers to call to ask questions or register a complaint. The stop card has been in use at Duke ever since.

5. On June 19, 1986, University of Maryland basketball star and All-American Len Bias died of cardiorespiratory arrest after using cocaine with teammates in their dorm room. The subsequent investigation revealed to national media scrutiny abuses in the Maryland basketball program so severe that athletic director Dick Dull and coach Lefty Driesell were forced to resign.

that have emerged from the twenty-fourth Summer Olympic Games,[6] I would hope that our way of playing the games at Duke will be a touchstone for you.

Find out what is wrong: discover the principles and values you should live by, then practice them in everyday life. In this year of presidential election I cannot help reminding you that, as important as it is to vote, voting is not enough. As historian Christopher Lasch observes, today "The responsibilities of citizenship have steadily dwindled, until they are exhausted by the simple act of casting a vote."[7] But good citizenship is about more than casting a vote; it is about taking your values with you wherever you go, into every area of your lives. Duke graduate David Bloom was an art history major who, indeed, loved art and knew a great deal about it. He became an investment advisor, but he loved art so much that he invested his clients' money in art and other beautiful things for himself. Apparently David Bloom was unable to take with him anything more than the ability to judge art and to possess it in private and self-centered enjoyment.[8] But his sense of right and wrong was no more connected to his investment skills and his remarkable knowledge of art than was any sense of right and wrong connected to Olympic athlete Ben Johnson's extraordinary gifts as a runner.[9]

6. Ten athletes were disqualified from competition after testing positive for banned substances at the 1988 Summer Olympics in Seoul, Korea.

7. Christopher Lasch, "Education as Public Ritual," *The Education Digest* (March 1986), 2.

8. In 1988 David Bloom, who graduated from Duke in 1985, was sentenced in New York to eight years in prison on one count each of mail fraud and securities fraud. Representing himself as an investment advisor (though he was unlicensed), Bloom took millions of dollars from clients which he then "invested" in an opulent lifestyle for himself, including a notable art collection, jewelry, travel, and luxury homes and cars.

9. Generally viewed as the worst of the 1988 Summer Olympics drug scandals

The great psychiatrist Robert Coles has observed that Americans in the latter half of the twentieth century appear to have disconnected their "personal values . . . moral ideals and ethical standards" from their "working lives"; we seem to feel, he says, that "we must not let our 'private morality' get in the way of what we do in our jobs."[10] You have been discovering your values here at Duke; when you leave here, live them. Take your values into every world you enter. Continue to find out what is wrong, and then find a way to do battle against it. It will be harder to persuade others to effect changes in corporate settings or in government. Yet, the First Amendment is alive and well out there in the free world, and the skills you have developed here to focus attention on what is wrong will still work. And with a Duke diploma on your wall, you know that people are going to be more willing to listen, for you come from an institution that leads the nation in addressing many of the wrongs in universities today.

We come now to rule 3: welcome the hard times. When you leave Duke you will make mistakes, you will take chances and you will occasionally fail. The lesson is not to stop taking chances; the lesson is not low self-esteem, not the notion that because you have taken a loss, you are therefore a loser. The lesson is to learn—to learn to take smarter and smarter, better informed chances; to learn to be more tolerant of other people's mistakes and failures as well as your own; and to learn humility. As a psychiatrist I can tell you that emotional maturity can only come from the experience of confronting our own fallibility and our vulnerability to the essential unfairness of life. Indeed, it is against this unfairness that I have urged you to struggle on behalf of others while

---

was the case of Canada's high-profile sprinter Ben Johnson, who after winning the 100-meter dash on Saturday, tested positive for the steroid stanozolol and was stripped of his gold medal the following Monday, September 26.

10. Robert Coles, "Our Moral Lives," *Society* (May/June 1986), 38.

you accept its lessons for yourself without bitterness. For in the acceptance as well as the struggle will be forged your finest qualities of character.

The lessons of pain and loss are the most important lessons you can learn, and they are, I fear, the ones we cannot teach in the classroom. You cannot get them by rote; you cannot get them by analysis; you cannot get them from the page or off the computer screen. Duke cannot include them in the curriculum, though I realize many of you have already encountered the beginnings of these lessons in your personal lives, and you may have seen this growth beginning in friends who have suffered. Or you may have glimpsed in your study of a historical or political figure something of the influence that personal tragedy brings to bear on the development of a great leader, a great thinker, an artistic genius who creates art out of inner pain and turmoil. Personal growth follows personal tragedy, and although time passes and the pain diminishes, fades, the spiritual learning remains for a lifetime.

Therefore, although I would like to wish you nothing but success when you leave Duke University, I cannot in good conscience do so, for it is the human experience of failure and loss that will ultimately be the source of greatest growth for you. What I wish for you after Duke is that you will become good students of life's humbling lessons, for then you will develop the understanding, the moral courage, and the strength to become the leaders and the heroes this nation needs.

I would like to conclude by summarizing this old advice for you. First, learn irrelevant things—and for the rest of your life anything can happen. Second, find out what is wrong—for by seeking to do what is right you will give meaning to your lives. And third, welcome the hard times—for if you face nothing but success, you will never learn courage and compassion.

And when you have connected these three things—when you have connected diverse knowledge with deeply held values and the understanding that comes from accepting the inevitable pain of human life—then you *will* be a genius: a genius at putting together a life you can be proud of, and that's as much as any of us can ever hope to achieve.

The Mechanisms of Hate

By 1987 campus watch articles in the popular press had shifted from deploring the "me generation" to reporting a new kind of civil rights awareness—on the one hand, what some observers described as an ugly backlash on the part of the white majority to affirmative action admissions policies at colleges and universities; and on the other, a concern, as pragmatic as it was idealistic, for greater understanding between majority and minority groups in an increasingly diverse student body. In response to a disturbing rise in reports of racist incidents and the harassment of women and homosexuals, American higher education turned to experiments with anti-harassment policies and speech codes, and orientation programs featuring "cultural diversity workshops."

At Duke we had been spared any violent or widely publicized incidents, but we knew full well that there was too much self-segregation by race on campus, that our gay community felt unwelcome, and that women's concerns for greater respect and safety needed to be addressed aggressively. Over the course of several years faculty committees sought and eventually agreed on a policy that provided workable guidelines and relief for both students and employees who felt they were being harassed. In the meantime, in the spring of 1989 a group of concerned students, administrators, and faculty discussed with the Duke community whether we should develop a speech code as had been done at Stanford, Michigan, Wisconsin, and other schools. Duke did not adopt such a code; consensus was quickly reached that freedom of speech remained the best protection and the best hope for all, and any restrictions would be especially detrimental, even ironic, at an educational institution. But our Office of Student Affairs did request that in my annual welcoming address to the first-year students in Duke Chapel, I specifically support a new orientation program then being developed.

My own experiences and the experience of Duke's peer institutions convinced me that real change in the campus climate was needed and that it would require not only the cooperation and good will of all constituencies, but also the public and determined support of the administration. For this speech, therefore, I drew on my background as a psychiatrist for explanations that might, in twenty-five minutes, reach a large group of excited eighteen-year-olds on a hot August day. Eventually, through the Chronicle of Higher Education *and the* Los Angeles Times *wire service, I reached a far larger, more mature audience than I had anticipated.*

ADDRESS TO THE CLASS OF 1993
DUKE UNIVERSITY
AUGUST 24, 1989

Each fall, faculty and students of Duke University assemble here to begin the year together in convocation, a symbol of our oneness as a community dedicated to the advancement of knowledge and truth. On behalf of this community I wish to welcome you, the class of 1993, and tell you that we have been looking forward to your energy, your optimism, your many hopes, and your high ideals. Our community needs these qualities in its citizens, and its citizens—you and I—must nurture in each other a productive idealism in the service of good citizenship if we are to combat the divisive elements that would threaten our community. It is on this subject that I wish to address you today.

There is a shadow that has fallen on our educational community—indeed, this shadow has swept across our nation. It is not new, but as our community has become increasingly more diverse, the shadow has darkened. I refer, of course, to the shadow of intolerance. You may have noticed in the news this past year that some frightening things have been happening on college and university campuses across the nation—things that students and faculties and administrators are trying to address together. One of these things is something journalists have taken to calling "The New Racism," and it involves students harassing and sometimes actually attacking other students on the basis of racial differences. In fact, instances of a wide spectrum of group intolerance appear to be increasing on campuses and include harassment on the basis of cultural and religious differences and harassment of students who are gay.

Another of the frightening things that are happening to college students is something that has always happened but that we did not have a specific name for until recent years—and until you can name a thing, it remains invisible. This thing we now call date or acquaintance rape is an act of both physical and psychological violence, and it is also one of the crudest and most violating aspects of sexism—the making of another person into an object on the basis of gender, to be used or abused in some way rather than respected as a fellow human being.

You have already received from me a preliminary introduction to these issues: a letter and a booklet entitled *Duke's Vision*[1] in which we begin exploring with you the meaning and importance of mutual respect and the understanding that multiculturalism

1. The twelve-page pamphlet was renamed *A Vision for Duke* in 1991 after some faculty objected to the title as an unwarranted assumption that everyone at Duke necessarily endorsed the vision as expressed. The pamphlet and a special program, first used as part of orientation in 1989, were developed by a committee of students, staff from our Office of Residential Life, and a professor from the Divinity School. The pamphlet expressed ideals of human community and gently exhorted new students to "reject stereotyping" and "strive to increase respect for the dignity of every human being. . . ."

is a desirable and enriching characteristic of the Duke community. Because we want you to learn to value the differences among you rather than being frightened or angered by them, we have arranged orientation workshops that will call your attention to your own attitudes and feelings about these differences and that will help us begin the process of exploring them together.

As you may know, I came to the presidency of Duke University from the profession of psychiatry and, of course, that training influences the way I think about and explain things. The orientation emphasis on the impact of differences will serve you well, I believe, as an introduction to the tensions that exist in a diverse community. But because of my background as a psychiatrist, I will address these issues of diversity from the other side, from the side of our essential likeness and what we all have in common—the implications, in other words, of our common humanity as opposed to the tensions of our many differences.

What is it, therefore, that racism and sexism and homophobia and religious and cultural intolerance have in common? They are all ways of denying that other people are of the same kind as we ourselves. This denial can be blatant, as in the hurling of ugly epithets or the physical harassment or coercion of another. Or it can be subtle and even unconscious, as when the contributions of some members of a group are consistently ignored or belittled. But whatever the manifestation and whoever the target may be, group hatred and suspicion arise from a primitive psychological mechanism that has nothing to do with the race, color, creed, gender, or sexual orientation of the excluded others.

Sadly, this is one of the basic characteristics that all of us human beings have in common: our inner-directed tendency to categorize and stereotype other groups of people as inferior to ourselves and to use them as scapegoats, as convenient objects of blame and animosity. Let me explain to you briefly, in terms of developmental psychology, how this mechanism of hate arises; for once we grasp that what we are seeing as objective reality may have been tampered with in fundamental ways by our subjective processes, we can begin to deal with others as individuals.

When you were an infant, your first laboratory assignment in becoming a human being was to discover that you and your mother were two separate entities. When you had completed this task successfully, you went on to discovering the boundaries between yourself and the other people around you, while at the same time, for the sake of species survival, you developed the ability to form strong family ties. Today this bonding capacity, learned as a child within the family, enables you to form strong friendships with others and eventually will enable you to form a new family of your own.

Paradoxically, this process which creates our species' ability to love also is the source of our ability to hate. The most commonly used example of this connection is the so-called recognition sequence observed in infants. Before you learned to distinguish your own mother from all others, you showed no fear of strangers. It was only when you recognized your bond with a particular mother that you then expressed fear and rejection of other people, embarrassing your family by screaming with terror at the approach of kind old Uncle Sigmund.

In the formation of groups, you and I—all human beings—duplicate the earliest conditions of our lives by this instinctual bonding mechanism that is necessary for species survival. But then, having formed groups for necessary and benign reasons, all too often—and for the most part unconsciously—human beings take the next step in the ancient sequence, the step that fears and rejects, that differentiates between the beloved familiar and the stranger, between the in-group and the out-group, between us and them.

To strengthen the bonding, the in-group identifies itself as superior to the out-group even where significant differences between the people involved are virtually nil. Then the in-group proceeds to defend this designated important difference as though it were a vital, objective reality rather than an inner, psychological choice. A recent psychiatric report on this phenomenon has characterized it as existing in a sort of "mental twilight zone" wherein we simultaneously hold the knowledge of our human kinship even as we fantasize our difference and superiority. Consider in this light the irony of Hitler's requirement that Jews wear the Star of David, without which these supposedly inferior others would have been indistinguishable from the rest of the German population.[2]

Now, how does all this relate to you, to your situation as Duke freshmen in the here and now? By describing the process of bonding and group formation, I am asking you consciously to see yourselves in a larger context, in the context of our history as a species and with a perspective that can help you to understand how important your experience with cultural diversity at Duke will be. We psychiatrists depend on a very important axiom in our work: that what is unconscious is not within a person's control, but what is once made conscious is thereby available for human beings either to understand, to change, or to reinforce. It is our hope that this week's orientation will alert you, will make you conscious of sometimes indulging in an in-group/out-group style of thinking. And when you realize that your reactions may have less to do with outer, objective reality and more to do with inner, psychological defense systems, we hope that you will stop and rethink and start asking questions, of yourself and of others. And then the challenge will be, of course, to take this knowledge and these new questions and act on them, act out of faith in our common humanity rather than fear of our differences, act individually and responsibly to change our behavior toward each other.

2. Group for the Advancement of Psychiatry, Committee on International Relations, *Us and Them: The Psychology of Ethnonationalism*, report no. 123 (New York: Brunner/Mazel, 1987), pp. 38, 103.

Because frankly, we—we as a species—can no longer afford our own infantile behavior. The human race has the power to blow up the world, and yet we continue to allow our actions, both personally and as nations, to be controlled by a psychological hate mechanism on autopilot. And all the while we vigorously maintain our own innocence of any wrongdoing. Like warring children we fiercely insist that it wasn't our fault, that the envied or feared "other" stepped over the imaginary line, "got on my side" and "made me do it." We project onto others—others of another color, of another creed, of another culture—our own fears, angers, imperfections; all the things about ourselves that we dislike we attribute to someone else, to the members of the out-group, even, at times, to people who simply happen to be of the opposite sex.

The great Swiss psychiatrist Carl Jung had a picturesque term for this psychological element commonly observed in human beings. He referred to it as the "shadow," the projection of each individual's darker side. Because it is so uncomfortable for us to acknowledge our own faults and recognize the possibilities for evil within our own natures, we repress the knowledge of our shadow and with relief turn it outward. "You can then," Jung writes, "at least say, without hesitation, who the devil is; you are quite certain that the cause of your misfortune is outside and not in your own attitude."[3]

It has been a troubling acknowledgment for this university—and for other American colleges and universities—to make, that in this privileged enclave where we talk about and think about and teach the lessons of humane learning, we have not necessarily been educating our community in attitudes of tolerance and humility. We have come to realize that we must be explicit, that the

3. Carl Jung, *The Structure and Dynamics of the Psyche*, vol. 8 in *The Collected Works of C.G. Jung*, trans. R. F. C. Hull, second edition, Bollingen Series XX (Princeton, N.J.: Princeton University Press, 1972), p. 272.

naturally broadening and civilizing process of a liberal arts education is not enough, by itself, to accomplish the goals of community we have set before us. We must engage intolerance and inhumanity openly and publicly, as a community, at every opportunity.

As Duke students your opportunity to help us accomplish these goals begins with orientation and will continue for the next four years as you choose the student organizations and the causes you will support. You have already heard, I am sure, about the opportunities for extracurricular activities at Duke, but it may not be clear to you that when we talk about the importance of extracurricular elements in your education, we are not talking about the importance of having a good social life. There are those students on this campus whose attitude will suggest that socializing is the main interest of a successful Duke student. These are the students who seem to feel compelled to minimize in their conversation any time spent in studying and whose outside interests appear to revolve around partying.

You should party. You should make friends. You should have fun. A disciplined life makes room for all your different selves. But do not be misled; you have much to lose by giving in to pressures that would trivialize commitment to your academic work or commitment to activities that address conditions of inequality, intolerance, harassment, or deprivation. When we talk about extracurricular opportunities, we are talking about adding another dimension to your education, a dimension that will permit you to learn leadership and organizational skills while encountering aspects of life that are not academic, that will permit you to acquire practical training in good citizenship by taking responsibility for the quality of life in your community right now. Therefore, when you select outside involvements, I urge you to find ways to pursue your interests and the development of these skills through projects that develop and nurture altruism—the unselfish concern for the welfare of others. This kind of emotional growth is as much a part of your Duke education as the curriculum for which you receive graduation credits, but it is the part of your education here that we leave entirely up to you. For better or worse, the choices you make of activities available at Duke to balance the time spent in studying can change the course of your life. You can make choices that will open your eyes to worlds and people and possibilities in yourself you never dreamed of, or you can make choices that will effectively deprive you of the education you seek today with so much excitement and the community you wish to join with so much good will.

In *Duke's Vision* you read that "with the return of each fall, a community which has been here for many years reconstitutes itself anew." We generally think of a community as having formed when people recognize not only their responsibilities to themselves, but their responsibilities to each other and to a common goal or set of beliefs. The class of 1993 is the single largest group of new citizens in our community. We invited you to join us because we believe you have something to contribute and because we believe that you have the ability to benefit from Duke. In other words, you have the capacity both to give and to receive, to teach and to learn, to influence others and to be influenced by them. We hold many hopes for you; may your education at Duke be all that you hope for as well.

The Tools of Democracy

One of the most divisive and vehement campus controversies during my eight years as president involved the student newspaper, the Chronicle. *I had become used to defending professors' First Amendment rights as the daily mail included a steady trickle of complaints about faculty whose views, whether spoken or in print, were offensive to various alumni and friends of the university. However, in the fall of 1991 I suddenly found myself defending students and then defending my defense of those students.*

On November 5 the Chronicle *carried a full-page advertisement, explicitly labeled as such and paid for by Bradley R. Smith of the Committee for Open Debate on the Holocaust at a California address. Under the headline "The Holocaust Controversy: The Case For Open Debate," Smith laid out a lengthy and carefully constructed argument that the Holocaust was a hoax, linking his case to the respectable scholarly pursuit of historical revisionism and claiming that the facts were being suppressed by "Thought Police" and advocates of political correctness on American campuses. This ad, clearly anti-Semitic in content though not in language, was being sent to college newspapers across the country. Some declined to accept it; among them were the papers at Harvard, Yale, Brown, the University of Pennsylvania, and the University of Southern California. Others decided to run the ad; among these were the newspapers at Cornell, Northwestern, the University of Michigan, Rutgers, and Duke.*

Publication at Duke, as at other schools, was immediately followed by a furor of protests. For those whose families had suffered in the Holocaust, the ad was felt as a painful insult. To others, it seemed not only offensive but dangerous, with its rational tone preying on the ignorant and the naive, propagating hate under the mantle of academic inquiry. The student editors who chose to accept the ad were publicly chastised by faculty, by other students, and by members of their own board as being irresponsible and insensitive, of helping to spread hatred and lies, of being dupes, of lacking journalistic integrity. On November 6, I issued a public statement deploring the content of the ad, calling on the community to use the occasion to "refute this terrible revision of history," and defending the student editors' decision:

> *Because at Duke we have come together to seek the truth, it seems especially shocking when blatant and potentially harmful untruths are circulated in our midst. It is tempting at such times to criticize those who by printing such an advertisement might wrongly be viewed as sponsoring the lies it contains. Yet to have suppressed these outrageous claims, offensive as they are, would have violated our commitment to free speech and contradicted Duke's long tradition of supporting First Amendment rights.*

This statement brought a further round of criticism directed at me, especially on the point of whether the First Amendment should be a consideration in the case of advertising. As emotions continued to run high, I issued a second statement on November 18 that said in part:

> *Some have suggested that the university should impose some form of administrative sanction on the paper or that its editors should be punished. . . . There are dissenting views among scholars on whether the* Chronicle*'s decision . . . relates directly or indirectly to the First Amendment or the values which undergird it. I am not an expert on the First Amendment, but I believe that for the university to take any action to control, penalize, or censor the student paper would clearly implicate the values secured by the First Amendment.*

As painful as the debate became, it led to a series of educational efforts by our faculty that fostered campus-wide discussion and learning about the Holocaust unprecedented in my memory at Duke. Meanwhile, mail criticizing the Chronicle*'s editors as well as my own statements and perceived inaction persisted both in the pages of the newspaper and on my desk. We did have our supporters within the Jewish community and on the Duke faculty. From our law school, in particular, I received expert encouragement from Dean Pamela Gann and noted scholars William Van Alstyne and Donald Horowitz. The trustees strongly supported both my condemnation of the ad and my refusal to impose sanctions on the independent student newspaper. In addition, every major newspaper in North Carolina took a very strong and supportive editorial position, and on December 21 the* Washington Post *also published a major editorial supporting Duke and Rutgers in their decisions to run the ad. In my private correspondence I frequently pointed out that the principal students involved in the decision to publish the ad were themselves Jewish and that their choice was a difficult one, made only after considerable thought. And finally, I noted, "The* Chronicle *does not create people like Bradley Smith, but it does reveal them for what they are."*

Explaining the university with an emphasis on its role as a special place of free inquiry was an almost daily part of my life while president. I performed this duty in letters and in speeches before many different audiences. In hindsight that fall of 1991, I was especially glad that I had chosen this recurrent theme for my first formal address of the academic year. It gave the students a preview of responsibilities—and complexities—to come.

ADDRESS TO THE CLASS OF 1995
DUKE UNIVERSITY
AUGUST 29, 1991

Each fall, faculty and students of Duke University assemble here in the chapel to begin the year together in convocation, a symbol of our oneness as a community dedicated to the advancement of knowledge. On behalf of this community I welcome you, the class of 1995.

Despite the hot weather, the burdens of unpacking, the certainties of getting lost, and the uncertainties of assigned roommates and new friends, you also, I know, have been looking forward to this day, to this arrival. For those of us who welcome you—for faculty, staff, and more experienced Duke students—your arrival marks the beginning of another school year of anticipated challenges and well known rewards. But for you, this is not just another year at school: this is the beginning of a whole new life. Therefore today we extend to you official greetings, recognizing and honoring you for the work that lies ahead. At the other end of this extended rite of passage, in the spring of 1995, the university community will gather once again in your behalf to say good-bye, recognizing and honoring you for your achievements, for the good use that you have made of our four years together.

These years of growth at Duke—the value of which depends so much on your own courage and initiative—nonetheless do not belong to you alone. They belong as well to our society, for the time allotted solely to learning is a special gift, an opportunity offered you, through this university, to prepare yourselves both intellectually and emotionally for the tasks of adulthood. Those tasks are three: meaningful work, meaningful relationships, and responsible citizenship—to work, to love, and to live in harmony with the human community. In truth, these tasks are inseparable; they must be pursued simultaneously, and simultaneously they will determine your goals, your values and commitments. Together they will create, inform, and represent your identity to the world. Work, love, and citizenship—your education at Duke must prepare you for all of these, must prepare you to study their complexities for the rest of your lives.

When you applied to Duke you may not have been thinking about your future and your education in all three of these ways. I think I can trust that you have given more than a little thought to your choice of academic studies, for all of you are excellent students. I am sure that you have devoted more than a little thought to making friends here and whether—or rather, when—you will fall in love. And your parents have certainly talked with you by now about your ultimate plans for a profession, though none of those plans can really be final, for the liberal arts have so much to offer you yet, not the least of which is knowledge of yourselves.

All this being the case, I thought we might spend our time together on the third element of your education at Duke, preparation for citizenship in this community, this nation, and the world. Our planet Earth is old, but according to statistical data from the United Nations,[1] its inhabitants are strikingly young: almost half the world's population today is below the age of twenty-five—some two and one-half billion young adults, adolescents, children, and infants. These are your peers and your younger sisters and brothers, the citizens of the world in which you will have much to do in the twenty-first century. One of the goals of your university education must be the development of a perspective that truly embraces this world, your world.

This is why I wrote to you back in July and sent you the booklet *A Vision for Duke*—so that you could begin developing the kind of broader perspective our increasingly complex world needs right here on the Duke campus. The ideals set forth in that booklet—ideals of justice, tolerance, and compassion—are goals that must serve the entire human community if we are to have any hope of stopping the ceaseless carnage characteristic of our species. To this day in our own country, where these values were literally written into the documents that created our governmental

1. Brian Urquhart and Erskine Childers, "Statistical Annex: Compilation of Statistical Data on UN Leadership Posts," in *A World in Need of Leadership: Tomorrow's United Nations* (New York and Uppsala, Sweden: Ford Foundation and Dag Hammarskjold Foundation, 1990), p. 23.

structure and political culture—in the Declaration of Independence, the Constitution, and the Bill of Rights—with these incomparable tools we continue to struggle to create a society that respects human dignity and grants equality to all, no matter the religion, the race, the ethnic heritage, the sexual orientation, or the gender of the individual human being.

The creation of such a society depends on each individual citizen who must determine for herself, for himself, that this principle of respect for others will be upheld whatever the tensions and strains may be. Balancing the rights of the individual and those of the group, the welfare of the individual and the welfare of the community—this is the dilemma that torments our country and makes it great. It is a dilemma we cannot, and in fact do not, want to protect you from while you are at Duke. For with increased personal freedom comes increased responsibility. We want you to enter fully into these concerns with us and help with working them out.

I know that you are aware of the ongoing public debate about America's identity as a multiethnic society. This debate is often framed in terms of fast-food metaphors for the brain—is this nation to be a melting pot or a tossed salad?—as if democracy were a great dining hall where the national appetite must choose between the fondue or the vegetable bar. As Duke is a university, not an "ivory tower" or a cafeteria, we enter the American debate at a somewhat higher level of discourse, at least most of the time. And we are bringing you into this debate as quickly as possible—right now, in fact, during orientation—because one of the university's responsibilities is to prepare you for citizenship in a democracy. So let us begin by framing in intellectual rather than gastronomic terms one of the large questions confronting our society: if our different racial and ethnic identities are pulling us apart, as some say they are, what can counteract those forces and hold us together?

I have suggested to you that a wider perspective, a sense of the world as your proper context, is vitally important. It will simply open your eyes. I have recently had my own point of view on democracy refreshed while reading a splendid book published just this year by a member of the Duke faculty, Professor Donald Horowitz of our Law School. His book, *A Democratic South Africa?*, looks at the conflict in that bitterly divided society and considers obstacles to and possibilities for the establishment of a democracy there. Viewing South Africa as the "quintessential challenge," Professor Horowitz notes that "The special problems of racially and ethnically divided societies require more than the usual measure of democratic ingenuity." What South Africa, for example, will require are "nonracial, nonethnic institutions . . . to serve [a] multiracial, multiethnic society. . . ."[2]

As I read Professor Horowitz's analysis of the difficulties facing South Africa, I was led to a deeper understanding of and appreciation for the sustained ingenuity of our own democracy and the miracle of its institutions and the freedoms they provide and protect. For these are the tools of democracy: our Constitution and our Bill of Rights and our twelve thousand newspapers;[3] our courtrooms and our legislatures, our public schools and our public libraries, the privacy of the voting booth and the inviolable privacy of individual conscience and religious belief. These are the tools of democracy that help and protect us despite our differences, that honor us in the midst of disagreement, that restore our dignity when we have been mean-spirited to one another.

It might be argued that the persistence of this predictably human meanness of spirit led James Madison, our fourth presi-

2. Donald L. Horowitz, *A Democratic South Africa? Constitutional Engineering in a Divided Society* (Berkeley: University of California Press, 1991), pp. xiii, 41.

3. According to the *Gale Directory of Publications and Broadcast Media*, 123d ed., ed. Karin E. Koek et al. (New York: Gale Research, Inc., 1991), pp. xxvi–xxvii, in the United States there are 11,689 daily, triweekly, semiweekly, weekly, biweekly, semimonthly, monthly, bimonthly, and miscellaneously published newspapers.

dent and the father of the Constitution, to the kind of insight that has made the difference for this nation. As a young man of twenty-two, about the age most of you will be when you graduate from Duke, Madison witnessed the persecution and imprisonment of a minority, a minority that in 1773 began voicing opinions and beliefs that were offensive to the establishment. Some historians have suggested that Madison may have been strongly influenced when he heard one of these dissenters "preaching" his unpopular views "unsquelched, from the jail."[4] This minority was the Baptists. Now we cannot help but recall the powerful message of Martin Luther King, also issued from a jail, and reflect that in 190 years some progress had been made: Dr. King was not jailed in 1963 in Birmingham for being a Baptist.

James Madison was not a Baptist, but he was a student who had read much about religion and about liberty and he had thought deeply about these matters. In the summer of 1776, when only twenty-five years old, he went as a delegate to Williamsburg where the Virginia Declaration of Rights was to be ratified. Article Sixteen concerned religious freedom. It said that all citizens "should enjoy the fullest Toleration in the Exercise of Religion according to the Dictates of Conscience." But James Madison Jr. objected. "Toleration" wasn't good enough. Historian William Lee Miller describes Madison at that time: "He was shy and short and new . . . and his voice was weak, but he was not going to let pass mere 'toleration.'" At college Madison had studied and debated the new revolutionary ideas with his teachers and classmates, including the idea that "toleration" implied "condescension," "some institution or belief in the superior position from which to do the tolerating," as Professor Miller explains.[5]

So "toleration" wasn't good enough; it had to be equality.

4. William Lee Miller, *The First Liberty: Religion and the American Republic* (New York: Alfred A. Knopf, 1986), p. 5.
5. Miller, p. 4.

And with the help of older, more influential delegates, Madison's amendment to the article was passed and thenceforward stated that all citizens "are equally entitled to the full and free exercise of religion, according to the dictates of conscience."[6] In 1785 Madison would have to defend religious freedom again in Virginia, and in 1789 he was one of the central figures in the writing of the First Amendment in which freedom of religion, freedom of speech, and freedom of the press are yoked forever to the service of our country and the protection of its citizens.

Let us recall, now, why I am telling you all this. We began by considering a question, the question of how to hold together a nation of minorities. For we are all in the minority in some way or the other, depending on where we are and whom we are with. By talking about James Madison I am suggesting one of the answers and an implement or tool whereby that answer might be put to work. Freedom of religion, freedom of conscience, freedom of speech—these are ways of talking about freedom of the human spirit. And is not freedom of the human spirit the one great principle around which all can rally? Is it not the most fundamental idea around which this nation was organized? James Madison certainly argued that it was the central idea, without which the entire American experiment would come unraveled, setting us on a "career of intolerance" that would lead once again to the "torrents of blood [that] have been spilt in the old world. . . ."[7] He began developing this conviction while at college. He explored it in the classroom, he read and heard what others had to say, and he related what he read and heard and thought about persecution and liberty to the life he saw around him. He concluded that those who are in the minority must be protected or the rights and free-

6. Miller, pp. 5–6.

7. James Madison, "Memorial and Remonstrance against Religious Assessments," in *The Papers of James Madison*, vol. 8, ed. Robert A. Rutland et al. (Chicago: University of Chicago Press, 1973), p. 302.

doms of all would be in jeopardy. He concluded that true equality would be needed to protect the freedoms that protect us all.

The tools of democracy have been preserved for you. They are ingeniously designed to serve you in all seasons and with every generation. Like the Bill of Rights and the Supreme Court and local elections, the university is also a tool of democracy, for we have found that knowledge and truth and open debate are the natural allies of freedom. Remember young James Madison at college and know how important your time in Duke classrooms will also be. Take up your tools and sharpen them. Begin the work of refashioning our institutions and examining our laws and customs with a critical eye that they might better serve our changing society.

This is not my idea, you know. I read it on one of the walls of the Jefferson Memorial in Washington, D.C. My main source of wisdom for today is James Madison, but as he was probably Thomas Jefferson's best friend, a word or two from our third president is appropriate. Thomas Jefferson believed in what he called "the progress of the human mind . . . [A]s new discoveries are made," he wrote, "new truths discovered and manners and opinions change with the change of circumstances, institutions must advance also to keep pace with the times."[8] We expect you to help Duke University keep pace with the times. You are the single largest group of new citizens in our community, and as such, your very presence has already begun to have an impact on this campus. What might you learn, what might you teach over the next four years that will further sharpen our tools of democratic idealism?

8. Jefferson Memorial, Southeast quadrant, Washington, D.C. Text in *Respectfully Quoted: A Dictionary of Quotations Requested from the Congressional Research Service*, ed. Suzy Platt (Washington: Library of Congress, 1989), pp. 38–39. Platt cites the original source as Thomas Jefferson, to Samuel Kercheval, July 12, 1816, *The Writings of Thomas Jefferson*, vol. 10, ed. Paul L. Ford (1899), pp. 42–43.

A traditional piece of Cherokee wisdom holds that leaders should "think about the impact of [their] decisions on seven generations into the future."[9] Thinking about the impact your education could have within the present generations alone is both overwhelming and exhilarating: What change of course might yet be accomplished for this tragic planet, with two and a half billion young minds and hearts at the helm? What cruelties and oppressions might this tidal wave of youth wash away? Only a few days ago we held our breaths as thousands of Soviet youths rushed unarmed to the defense of the Russian parliament. Our own news correspondents marveled: "The pride and defiance seemed greatest," one wrote, "among people in their teens and twenties."[10] Another tells the story of a little independent newspaper started in Moscow by young people just out of college. After only a year of experience with freedom of the press, they literally risked their lives during the coup to publish the truth. "There was no other answer," said one, "for the democracy of our country." Said another, "Our strength was in the newspaper that we gave to the people."[11]

Thanks to *glasnost*, these young people must have known about the blood of students on Tiananmen Square. But this time the courage of youth was enough to stop the tanks, and in the early hours of last Thursday morning we heard the halting words of a translator conveying President Boris Yeltsin's tribute: "What is symbolic," he said, "is that those who protected the Constitution were many young people. This is a sign," he went on to explain, that the undertaking of freedom in the Soviet Union will suc-

9. Wilma Mankiller, chief of the Cherokee Nation of Oklahoma, "She Leads a Nation," interview by Hank Whittemore, *Parade Magazine*, August 18, 1991, 4–5.
10. Fred Hiatt, "Coup Resisters 'Not Heroes, but We Are Patriots,'" *Washington Post*, August 22, 1991, A1, A27.
11. Laurie Hays, "'Our Strength Was in the Newspaper We Gave to the People,'" *Wall Street Journal*, August 22, 1991, A1, A6.

ceed.[12] Looking out at you this morning—if not billions or thousands, nevertheless an impressive crowd—I cannot believe that our own nation is today in less courageous hands. The dangers to our democracy are perhaps more subtle than armored divisions and Molotov cocktails, but they are just as real. They are mean-spirited dangers, of hatred and intolerance, and they are also dangers of neglect and thoughtlessness and ignorance. But you have the advantages of being born into the habit of democracy and of being given time to learn more about its complexities.

I said at the beginning of this talk that your education at Duke should prepare you for the three tasks of adulthood: to work fruitfully, to love responsibly, and to live in harmony with the human community. I also said that your growth toward these goals would proceed simultaneously. During the coming year you will search eagerly for the right answer to every question you encounter. You will debate late into the night with friends and during the day with professors who make you angry because they insist on questioning everything. You will become frustrated. As a sophomore you may be cynical: since everything can be questioned, nothing means anything. Meanwhile friends will have failed you and you will be disappointed in the way some people behave.

Fortunately, this dismal state of affairs will not last. By your junior year intellectual growth will have brought you to a greater level of comfort with the gray areas of ideas and of people. You will see that virtually every answer raises another question, and you will be able to tolerate this, and you will also be able to tolerate the differences and changes in people. By your senior year it will have occurred to you that perhaps you occasionally disappoint others yourself, and you will have begun making choices among ideas and possibilities by weighing the evidence and con-

12. "Russian President Boris Yeltsin Remarks to the Russian Parliament," 5:15 a.m. ET (approx.), August 22, 1991, Moscow, Reuter's Transcripts, CQ's Washington Alert.

sidering the consequences. At this point you will have begun to develop a real capacity for commitment: to your work, to other people (especially one significant other person), and finally, to values which you have been developing for yourself all along.[13] And your commitment to these values will determine the quality of your citizenship—whether you will look beyond yourselves to the greater good of our society and our world.

Perhaps you will decide, like James Madison, that freedom for others is just as important as freedom for yourself. Perhaps you will risk jail for freedom of the press like the young reporters for Moscow's *Independent Newspaper.* Or quietly, in your everyday life, support the rights of others to speak their conscience no matter how controversial their views. Someday you will surely be called upon to protect our Constitution—in a courtroom, at the polls, in a town council meeting, or through a grassroots organization—just as the young people of the Soviet Union last week protected theirs in the streets of Moscow; just as an earlier generation of young Americans once protected it in the streets of cities like Birmingham and Greensboro and Washington. For now, you are called on to practice your citizenship at Duke University as part of an education that will lead to the commitments of a lifetime. I can wish you no better preparation, no more important journey, than the four years that lie ahead.

13. This phase of development is usefully summarized in *Friends and Lovers in the College Years,* formulated by the Committee on the College Student, Group for the Advancement of Psychiatry (New York: Mental Health Materials Center, 1983), pp. 18–21. GAP draws on William G. Perry, *Forms of Intellectual and Ethical Development in the College Years* (New York: Holt, Rinehart, & Winston, 1968).

Children of the Cold War

As I thought about my final welcoming address to new students, I was struck by how dramatically the world outside the university's gates had changed since 1985 and the ways in which the impact of these changes was felt at Duke. While the campus continued to be a relatively protected environment, a valuable time-out for young people on the verge of adulthood, very real issues of personal safety and group responsibility had now to be laid explicitly before our students for discussion and for action. Accordingly, between the fall of 1985 and the fall of 1992, new student orientation week had changed dramatically at Duke as it had at most of our peer institutions. To the usual chores of picking up room keys, wrestling boxes and bags into dormitories, and meeting with academic advisors (tasks doubtless unchanged in substance since Trinity College opened its doors in Durham in 1892), were added self-defense workshops and mandatory health information sessions. In 1992 new students were also required to attend an assembly where famed author and actress Maya Angelou breathed life into the already clichéd term "multiculturalism" via an inspirational message drawn from personal experience; to participate in the Class of 1996 Community Service Outreach Day, which introduced new students to the reality of social problems in our surrounding urban community; and to see Sounds Dangerous, *a play performed by Duke students about sexual assault and alcohol abuse on campus.*

Safety gradually became as important a campus community theme as cultural diversity and voluntarism. More and more, we had to accept that Duke Forest and our beautifully tended gardens and grounds were no barrier to the encroachment of urban crime. In 1989, in response to assaults on employees and students, I appointed a safety task force to find both immediate and long-term solutions. Along with increasing patrols by Duke Public Safety officers, expanding escort services, and educating students and staff about prevention, we added emergency outdoor telephones and additional lighting and installed coded electronic door-locking devices in academic buildings and dormitories.

But equally important to solve for safety's sake were the problems posed by our students' own youth and inexperience, especially in regard to alcohol and sex. As we began to see some students and faculty turn HIV positive and ultimately come down with the clinical syndrome of AIDS, we developed a program to promote awareness of risk factors, provided for "super-confidential" AIDS testing, and arranged for condom distribution in the dorms. Possibly the most significant step taken during my presidency to address the safety concerns of our women students in the long term was the creation of a women's center to coordinate activities in support of women and to focus attention on such issues as date rape. To supplement other university programming, I allocated $10,000 *annually for rape education to be conducted by the center and the student group DARE (Duke Acquaintance Rape Education). The Duke Women's Center, under the leadership of its first director, Martha Abshire Simmons, successfully provided psychological support and education for the entire community, and, through its Safe Haven program, offered physical support by staying open late on weekend nights for women who felt threatened or who had had too much to drink.*

To prepare our students for a community that was more hostile than Duke's pastoral campus might suggest, we had asked the Office of Student Affairs to orchestrate special programs introducing them to the opportunities, the problems, and the resources of Duke and Durham. Mine was now the task of explaining what orientation themes of cultural diversity, personal development, and community responsibility had to do with the rest of the world.

ADDRESS TO THE CLASS OF 1996
DUKE UNIVERSITY
AUGUST 27, 1992

Each fall it is our custom to open the academic year with a special welcome to the first-year students because you are the largest group of new citizens in our community and, for the most part, you are the youngest. This means that, among all of us at Duke today, the possibilities for you are the greatest—the possibilities for achievement, for happiness, for making a difference in the world. This morning we greet the class of 1996, 1,630 new beginnings, and we rejoice with you in all the good work of growth and learning that lies ahead.

You are the last entering class that I will greet as president of Duke University. I wish to mention this so as to acknowledge with you that today is a special point of reference for both of us. August of 1985 was the first time I considered how best to welcome and advise new students. The members of the entering class that year were much like you: among the brightest in the country, from diverse backgrounds, with an extraordinary variety of talents and achievements to enrich this community. As a class you and they clearly have those things in common. But in at least one important respect you are different, and this is why part of the message I share with you today must also be different.

Some advice, however, is worth repeating. As a psychiatrist I want to reassure you about one of the characteristic stresses of college life—the balance you must achieve between the slow, imperceptible process of intellectual growth and discipline on the one hand, and on the other, the dramatic, often risky involvements of your emotional journey to maturity. Many times over the next four years you will wish that somehow your personal lives could be put on hold until your academic goals have been achieved, or that your course work could be laid aside while your personal relationships are sorted out. But as the Spanish philosopher Ortega has expressed it, "Life is fired at us point-blank. . . . We cannot put off living until we are ready."[1]

During your years of baccalaureate study at Duke, you will feel pulled in opposite directions by the requirement to develop simultaneously a capacity for intimacy and a capacity for isolation. It may help if you realize that, psychologically, these are the developmental tasks of your age. To achieve true intimacy you must learn to relate to other human beings on a mature and responsible emotional level and you must care enough about yourselves that you can respect and allow another person's interest in you. To achieve a capacity for isolation, you must develop the ability to tolerate being alone, recognizing that you are an individual, separate and slightly different from all others.

The reality of your lives as students will require that you study in isolation much of the time. The importance of your ability to tolerate this state in order to learn effectively cannot be overemphasized. And even as you isolate yourself with your books, you will be enhancing your capacity for close friendship, for the ability to be alone is a prelude to the development of intimacy. The student who must always be surrounded by friends, who depends upon others for the discipline to study, who always requires an audience, may never develop the maturity of personality required in an adult world.

Another piece of durable advice, just as relevant today as it was then, is this: whatever else happens in your lives over the next four years—and much will happen, I know: examinations will be passed or failed, roommates will work out or they won't, parents may or may not send money, friends might wreck cars, friends certainly will break hearts—whatever else happens to you at Duke, please, get your education. Get the full value of your investment here by pursuing aggressively the opportunities for

1. José Ortega y Gasset, *Mission of the University,* trans. Howard Lee Nostrand (Princeton, N.J.: Princeton University Press, 1944), p. 84.

learning this university offers you, opportunities no other place in your lives will ever duplicate. Don't arrive at Wallace Wade Stadium on graduation day with regrets about the real meaning of the degree you have earned. I am reminded that in one of our greatest works of autobiography, the grandson of two American presidents looked back on his own undergraduate education as a waste. As a mature man Henry Adams regretted that while a college student he had been influenced by those who did not grasp the excitement of learning. Of himself as a student Henry Adams recalled that he did not go off to college wanting only "one per cent of an education. He regarded himself," Adams wrote, "as the only person for whom his education had value, and he wanted the whole of it. He got barely half of an average."[2]

Don't settle for barely half of what you have come for. You are very bright, it's true, bright enough to realize that with only an average expenditure of effort you can earn a diploma. But do you really want only an average amount of knowledge, a mere percentage of the learning that could be yours? You are the person for whom your Duke education has the greatest value. Please do not lose sight of this fact or of the realization that after twelve years of schooling chosen for you by the adults in your life, you have chosen four years at Duke University. Don't disappoint yourself; make the most of it.

In summary form, then, that's what I spent approximately twenty minutes saying to the first class I ever welcomed to Duke. I have shared the best of it with you this morning because, as I look back, it is clear that some concerns of student life never change. But I need to add to these topics something more, an aspect of your education that did not seem so urgent back then, something that you and I must now address together. That first

2. Henry Adams, "Harvard College," chap. 4 in *The Education of Henry Adams, an Autobiography* (Boston: Houghton Mifflin Co., Riverside Press Cambridge, 1927), p. 59.

speech focused on an internal world, the world of the students' individual psyches and the world of their new home, this campus. It seemed then that there would be time later to consider the rest of the world, that there was time now for a bit of the "ivory tower," because the world outside our gates seemed to permit it, seemed to be prosperous and stable enough to allow our students a temporary reprieve.

I am not suggesting that 1985 was in any sense "the good old days," in any way a simpler time—far from it. But in August of 1985 Duke students had every reason to believe that the world would pretty much rock along the way it always had while they went about the business of getting an education, and that when they graduated there would be a good job waiting and a world filled with problems and bad guys in a shape, size, quantity, and assortment they could easily recognize.

And so we come to the difference between you and them: they were the children of the Cold War, and you are not. They were the children of an expanding American economy and a world divided into predictable "third's": the Third World, the Free World, and the Communist world. Theirs was a world conveniently divided by a durable metaphor, the Iron Curtain, and by that metaphor made concrete, the Berlin Wall. When they applied to Duke as high school seniors, the greatest threat to American life seemed to emanate from a so-called "Evil Empire" somewhere far away from their own lives and concerns.

Then that world changed, almost literally overnight: in 1986, *glasnost*, freedom of expression in the Soviet Union; in 1987, *perestroika*, restructuring of the Soviet economy. In 1989 the most poignant symbol of the Cold War, the Berlin Wall, was dismantled. As the USSR gradually dissolved, our gigantic defense industry, frequently described as one of the pillars of our economy, could be justified no more than the us-versus-them worldview we had relied upon for so long. Suddenly we realized that the greatest threat to America was not so far away after all, that the greatest threat lay within our own borders, rooted in our differences of race, of wealth, and of culture. In the words of a wise comic strip character named Pogo, we had met the enemy and it was us.

This is why your orientation to Duke will include a serious and focused look at the issues and the tensions created by a diverse community. In one sense the Duke community might be considered homogeneous: we are all here for the purpose of education, either to pursue it or to support it. And we are all of the same kind—humankind, that is. Unfortunately, we human beings have a way of escalating the far less important matter of our differences to murderous proportions. Day after day the evidence accumulates before our eyes in television and newspaper reports and pictures, showing us that the "new world order" may prove to be even more cruel—and more dangerous—than the old.

The demise of Communist repression has resulted paradoxically in outright war among ethnic groups. In Yugoslavia, for example, where the bonds of oppression have been lifted, underlying racial and religious tensions have erupted into civil war. One can only surmise that long held prejudice and intolerance lay smoldering under Communism, that these attitudes were passed down through the generations and now see expression through atrocities so grievous as to make one wonder at the price Yugoslavia is paying for its newfound freedom. In the tragic African nation of Somalia we see a total breakdown of government and barbarism so rampant as to cause the mass starvation of thousands of innocent citizens while warring clans battle desperately in what they perceive as their only chance for survival.

The carnage in Somalia seems very far away to us this morning, but that is an illusion; Somalia is only as far away as Los Angeles. Yes, I am exaggerating—the tragedy in Africa dwarfs anything our nation has suffered internally since the War Between the States. But there is a troubling strand of similarity between the circumstances leading up to the L.A. riots[3] and those that obtained in Somalia during twenty-one years of dictatorship. The executive director of the human rights organization Africa Watch, Rakiya Omaar, has described these conditions in a recent report. First, the government of Somalia outlawed any private celebration that encouraged or acknowledged ethnic heritage in an attempt to stamp out what was termed the "scourge of tribalism." As a psychiatrist I can tell you that this attack on one of the fundamental bases of human identity had a predictable outcome: the people of Somalia were alienated from any sense of national community and clung ever more tightly to their ethnic pride as a matter of personal survival. Few among us would react any differently. Second, the government in Somalia gradually destroyed the civil institutions whereby people's grievances could be heard and their conflicts fairly resolved. With no trusted framework left to them for peaceful change or meaningful political dialogue, the people turned to violence.[4]

The lesson to be drawn from Somalia and applied to Los Angeles is obvious: when people feel that their ethnic heritage is not respected, that their racial pride is devalued or treated as a negative force; when they believe their civic institutions are failing them, are not being fair—as was the case with the Los Angeles police force and the courts—then they will erupt in violence. This is the legacy of oppression and always will be. And this is the broad context—the worldwide context—for our special program of orientation, A Vision for Duke.

Respect for human life, respect for human dignity, for the com-

3. On April 29, 1992, widespread violence erupted in Los Angeles when the four L.A. police officers accused in the brutal beating of black motorist Rodney King were acquitted by a Ventura County Superior Court jury.

4. Rakiya Omaar, "Somalia: At War with Itself," *Current History, a World Affairs Journal* (May 1992), 230–34.

mon thread that unites all of humankind, seems far too scarce in the world as you begin your college days. And so, as the first step in your Duke education, we bring before you these issues of racial and cultural tension and the responsibilities of community. Not so long ago American colleges and universities—Duke among the rest—took it for granted that our students would gradually absorb, with their liberal arts educations, enough knowledge of other cultures and sufficiently open attitudes to become the effective leaders of the next generation. And we assumed that the increasingly diverse communities on our campuses, reflective of a changing nation and a changing world, would create and recreate themselves without any special guidance or preparation—that our common goals and our good will would be sufficient.

But national and international uncertainty have increased, swiftly and inextricably, and the need for a new consciousness has become urgent. Last month, in response to the pressing questions raised for America in a radically altered world, the Carnegie Endowment released the report of a distinguished bipartisan national commission. Their many pages of careful analysis conclude with two fundamental recommendations. First, we must get our own house in order. As the commission states it: "We must make real for our own people the values we champion on the international scene." At the same time, we must reorient the education our young people receive. Again, to quote from the report: "The new kind of American leadership . . . must rely on a sophisticated knowledge of the world and sensitivity to the perspectives of other nations."[5]

Clearly, a sensitivity to other perspectives must begin at home. This is why we have chosen to be explicit about our hope to nur-

5. Carnegie Endowment National Commission on America and the New World, *Changing Our Ways* (Washington, D.C.: Carnegie Endowment for International Peace, 1992), pp. 85, 87.

ture in you a tolerance for differences. We are asking directly for your help in softening the prejudices you bring to Duke. We are asking you to consciously examine the unconscious baggage that gets in the way of enjoying and learning from others. In the end, I hope that the Duke community will kindle in you a belief that the differences among us are far less important than our common humanity.

The breakdown of this faith in Los Angeles was a tragic warning that we cannot go about our daily business oblivious to conditions that diminish the lives of others. In the days following the L.A. riots, I was moved to read the following words of a dedicated American leader:

> In this difficult day, in this difficult time for the United States, it is perhaps well to ask what kind of a nation we are . . . [we] can be filled . . . with hatred toward one another. Or we can make an effort . . . to understand and to comprehend. . . . [W]hat we need in the United States is not hatred; what we need in the United States is not violence . . . but love and wisdom, and compassion toward one another, and a feeling of justice toward those who still suffer within our country. . . .[6]

These are not, however, the inspiring words of a living American leader spoken in the wake of the Rodney King verdict. They are the words of Robert Kennedy spoken on the day that Martin Luther King was assassinated. Nearly a quarter of a century later we are still struggling to understand and to comprehend, to keep faith with one another.

6. Quote found in David Murray, "Timely Words from the Past," *Berkshire Eagle* (Pittsfield, Mass.), May 7, 1992, A9. See also Jules Witcover, *85 Days: The Last Campaign of Robert Kennedy* (New York: William Morrow Quill Edition, 1988), pp. 140 ff.

And so, from now on, we will ask a great deal of you because you are the children of a new era—an era yet to be defined. If there is to be a new world order, an enlightened world order, it will be the new world that you and your classmates shape and defend. May your time on this campus empower each of you to become the influence for justice and compassion we so sorely need.

What It Means to Be a Duke Athlete

Throughout my presidency one of the most publicly visible and appreciated series of developments related to the emergence of our athletic department as a national presence. Our first National Collegiate Athletic Association championship was won by the men's soccer team in 1986, the same year Coach Mike Krzyzewski's basketball team became national contenders. Having played their way to the Final Four in 1986, 1988, 1989, and 1990, they won national championships in 1991 and 1992 as well as nationwide respect and fame for Duke's commitment to the integrity of the student athlete. We established a women's soccer team in 1988, which in 1992 made it all the way to the NCAA championship game. Men's and women's tennis and golf, volleyball, field hockey, lacrosse, fencing, and wrestling all began to bring home Atlantic Coast Conference championships and invitations to participate in NCAA tournaments. Even football tied for the ACC championship and received a bowl invitation in 1989. By 1992 Duke hats and shirts were as likely to be seen in New York or Seattle as they were in Durham.

My father had warned me when we first talked about the Duke presidency that I had no understanding of sports. Prior to assuming the chancellorship, I had never been to a football or basketball game. During high school and college, when my peers were on the field, I was occupied with books and test tubes and tympani. I never even read the sports pages. In the spring of 1986, near the end of my first academic year as president, I was asked to address the senior athletes. This speech, given annually thereafter, became for me a benchmark of my growth in awareness. As my understanding evolved, so did my remarks. I offer here an emendation of the 1993 text, omitting several pages of praise for individual and team performance for the year.

ADDRESS TO THE SENIOR ATHLETES
DUKE UNIVERSITY
APRIL 26, 1993

One of the unexpected pleasures of my presidency has been the unique opportunity this office has afforded me—the opportunity for a nonathlete to know something of intercollegiate competition from the inside. Thus, I have come to understand your world through the eyes of a psychiatrist. What I have observed in the locker rooms, on the field, in the stadiums, are the remarkable attributes of dedication, discipline, and altruism that you demonstrate consistently throughout your seasons.

You may not realize it, but through your wins and losses and by the way you have balanced both academic and athletic challenges, you have helped define Duke University; you have truly demonstrated what intercollegiate sports and college athletics should be. As a class you have supported and strengthened the tradition of the student athlete at Duke. I know this to be the case because each year I ask to see the academic record of our graduating athletes. The number of you who have made dean's list or dean's list with distinction, who have been named academic all-Americans or won postgraduate scholarships or been accepted into rigorous professional and graduate programs at other universities; your membership in academic honor societies (including Phi Beta Kappa) and your place on the ACC Honor Roll all attest not only to superior personal achievement, but also to the quality and integrity of the peer group, whose members set high standards of performance and personal conduct for each other in the classroom, on the field or court, and in your private lives. Surely it has been your individual commitment to both scholastic and athletic achievement that has provided the intangible but important support for teammates that makes the crucial difference.

Your contests are so public, so visible, that they serve well to display not only physical courage and skill, but also the many virtues of the human spirit. The determination to excel, perseverance, and the willingness to make personal sacrifices have shaped your characters. You have faced disappointments, yet when bad luck strikes in any of your sports, you sustain each other's morale, taking pride in individual performance. A tough season is hard to overcome, yet you never let hardships tear you apart or weaken the bonds developed through shared experience, outstanding play, and close games. Ultimately, these difficult seasons add perhaps even more to your maturing than do your victories. Probably no one hates to fail as much as an athlete, yet you live not only with the fear of public failure at every game or meet, but also with the possibility of injury, and you do not let it hinder you. This reservoir of personal strength will serve you well in years to come, for your experiences as a Duke athlete have been those that you needed most at this time in your life. When you have won a point or a game, achieved a personal goal, you have seen that hard work and discipline do pay off, that you can influence the course of events through your own efforts, and that developing a special talent carries with it innate rewards that belong to you forever.

For those who are younger, the example you have set is compelling as you assume an influence larger than life on your youthful fans. At every game or match or meet of the season, Duke athletes are providing children with someone to look up to, a hero to emulate, and a sense of possibilities for the future. At a time when intercollegiate athletics is stained by controversy, when crimes of violence and problems of drug abuse seem to dominate the news of our youth, what a marvelous balance for our nation's youngsters—to see the results of discipline and practice, to watch you, our Duke athletes, bringing out the best in each other. At a time when the world cries out for heroism, when valor, self-sacrifice, and wholeness of spirit seem wanting, you bring these virtues to the fore and wear them as publicly and proudly as you have worn your Duke blue and white.

How proud we are of your stamina, spiritual as well as physical! You have earned our admiration for all your contributions—to your sport, to your university, and to the uniquely American ideal of the student athlete that requires you to be champions in the classroom as well as in the games. We are proud that you have pursued excellence in your sport as part of a liberal arts education. Just as you have studied history and poetry and the elegance of mathematical equations for their own sakes, for the intellectual growth and enrichment they bring, so also have you proven yourselves as competitive athletes for the sheer joy of developing one of those special talents that set you apart. What a paradox is here: through dedication to the games, you have had the opportunity to become better people, more mature, more courageous, with greater potential for compassion beyond the boundaries and experiences of your own lives. Because you are superb athletes who have pushed your bodies to the limit, you can have empathy for the person who must struggle with physical limitations. Because you have tried your best and yet lost to opponents, you can respect others who try and fail. Because you have disciplined yourselves over the long term, gradually building the strength to win, you can inspire those who must battle daily against the odds.

How much you have to share as you leave us and go out into the world! Wherever you go, whatever you do, your career as a Duke athlete will remain an important part of what you have to offer others. I hope you will draw consciously on these experiences as a source of strength and always remember that every one of you is a hero and a role model to the young people who have seen you play. When you can, I urge you to continue to help those who follow you by volunteering through your sport. You have special powers to teach our children the lessons of achievement through self-discipline, fair play, and the courage to keep on trying. Pass on the secrets of success in life that your Duke coaches and teammates have taught you.

In a few weeks when you leave here to go on to positions of influence and wider responsibilities that henceforth will define you to the world, you will be described by the phrase "former Duke athlete." I know you will continue to make us proud.

4

ADDRESSING FACULTIES

Tradition and Progress: The Expectations of Universities in Highly Industrialized Countries

In October of 1985 I agreed to a two-year term as liaison between the Association of American Universities (AAU) and the Standing Conference of Rectors, Presidents and Vice-Chancellors of the European Universities (CRE). The organization comprises some 360 members from institutions of higher education and research in twenty-three countries. I accepted this role for two reasons. First, it offered me an opportunity to act both personally and officially to further one of the goals set forth in my inaugural address—to internationalize the university at a greater rate. Second, I knew I could count on the advice and support of two of Duke's most respected leaders: former chancellor and dean of our law school Kenneth Pye (who left Duke in 1987 to accept the presidency of Southern Methodist University), and R. Taylor Cole, a distinguished political scientist, former provost, and the founder of international studies at Duke.

My assignment for the fall 1986 CRE meeting in Madrid was to speak on the general theme of international cooperation from the point of view of the American research university, or rather—as stated in my charge—the European university was to be "confronted with its counterparts in other regions of the world." The general nature and weightiness of this topic seemed daunting, but Ken Pye insisted that Duke's overseas presence would be boosted if I took this opportunity "to make a good impression for Duke before a hundred university presidents from approximately twenty countries." More important was his point—one that Taylor Cole had been talking to me about as well since my days as chancellor—that the creation of a trans-Atlantic dialogue on common problems of education would be of real significance for all of us. A rising tide of nationalism among the universities of Europe; isolationist sentiments on the part of some parents, who feared that American students in study-abroad programs might land in a backwash of terrorism; the Cold War, which denied academic freedom to the scholars and scientists of Eastern Europe, effectively cutting them off from timely information in their fields of study; financial problems caused by decreased government funding of higher education on both sides of the Atlantic; and the good news of an increasingly global economy and a technological revolution that all universities might benefit from if we would but pool our ideas, expertise, and experience—these were challenges that personal contact, talking and sharing, could address to good effect, I felt sure.

The CRE conference in Madrid was attended by more than 200 representatives of major European universities on both sides of the Iron Curtain and by guests from industry and commerce. I came away from the intense three days of meetings convinced that the interface between the AAU and CRE should be continued and expanded. American universities had advanced technologies to share, while European faculties and students could, through exchange programs, bring to American campuses not only their knowledge, but also the invaluable tonic of their sharply different worldviews. In addition to providing the occasion for valuable contacts with my European counterparts, my speech included at least one section that proved to be of durable value. I reported on Duke's new policy for industry-sponsored research, revised at a time when funding patterns for federally supported basic research were shifting in the United States and European universities were just beginning to negotiate cooperative ventures with industry. Throughout my presidency research partnerships between U.S. business and higher education of necessity proliferated, and I found myself going to the files again and again for requested copies of the explanations originally prepared for Madrid.

ADDRESS TO THE COUNCIL OF EUROPEAN RECTORS
MADRID, SPAIN
OCTOBER 23, 1986

The universities of the world exist today in a place of tension between society's immediate needs and the age-old search for knowledge and truth that created Western civilization. In our time as in all times, the universities are the essential institutions; our civilization is balanced precariously on the agreement of a frequently beleaguered and tragically divided world community of scholars—a community that is our responsibility to mend and to lead.

One of America's highly respected university presidents once remarked on the fact that eighty-five institutions established in the Western world by 1520 still exist in recognizable form, their fundamental purposes unchanged. And of that eighty-five, seventy are universities.[1] I have always remembered his point because of the sense of hope it gives me for our future and the sense of pride that American higher education, though comparatively young, can claim to share in the long tradition of these European institutions because they were the template of our American universities. And yet, from this perspective of centuries-old stability, the university seems an anomaly today, a deviation from what has become the common rule of political turmoil, swift change upon change, and an increasingly fragmented worldview. Historically, the stance of the university has been to see itself as part of a whole world and to maintain itself as an institution in a constant relation to society. Ours is a place simultaneously cloistered and dynamic, serving both the short- and long-term interests of our world. We are charged with living by two clocks: one, the frantically ticking time bomb of contemporary life; the other, the slow

1. Clark Kerr, *The Uses of the University* (Cambridge: Harvard University Press, 1982), p. 152.

and ritual sands of human history. Any significant failure on our part to balance these two responsibilities—to meet immediate societal needs while protecting the freedom of the human mind to range far and deep—will further imperil an already bitterly divided world.

As your offspring American colleges and universities continue to share not only the traditional commitment to basic research and academic freedom, but the problems of meeting society's most pressing needs. You and I are both feeling the pressure to contribute our resources more directly to an increasingly competitive world economy, to address the employment concerns of our young people, to cope with projected enrollment declines and our own increasing financial needs even as governments cut back funding while the costs of equipping sophisticated research labs continue to rise. Unfortunately, I think it is fair to say that on both sides of the Atlantic we pursue solutions to these problems with little or no reference to the experience of universities in other parts of the world—as if no problem in education which is troubling us individually could possibly have been usefully confronted or pondered on any other part of the globe. The ability of human beings to pay themselves the compliment of benign insularity is truly a thing to wonder at. Recently one of Duke University's most respected scholars shared with me what he considered to be the best current bibliographic essay on international studies. On the author's list of a dozen key international journals in the field of higher education, I was disappointed and embarrassed to see that not one is published in the United States.[2]

Certainly this is a matter for more than academic embarrassment, and I am pleased to be able to tell you that there are encouraging signs of an increased international awareness at America's

2. Philip G. Altbach, *Perspectives on Comparative Higher Education: A Survey of Research and Literature*, Occasional Paper, no. 16 (Princeton, N.J.: International Council for Educational Development, 1985), p. 52.

colleges and universities. According to our most recent survey of campus trends, four in ten American colleges and universities are currently seeking new ways to increase their offerings in international studies. This trend comes in response to what we have come to call the reform reports of 1984 and 1985, in which the academic programs of our nation's colleges and universities were heavily criticized for having drifted too far from the rigor of the traditional liberal arts curriculum. The reports noted an overemphasis on vocationalism in response to student demands and an overspecialization in teaching interests among faculty. Happily, these blue-ribbon committees of America's foremost educators also achieved a consensus that international and multicultural experiences should be numbered among the nine elements essential for a liberal undergraduate education in the United States. Unhappily, the commitment to international experiences for institutions of higher education themselves must be nurtured from a fairly low point: only about three in ten American colleges and universities today have established linkages with institutions abroad and only 21 percent provide overseas experiences for their faculty.[3]

When I came into office as president of Duke University, I pledged my institution to a larger role as an international university. I was greatly influenced in my decision by Dr. David Hamburg, a fellow psychiatrist and president of the Carnegie Corporation, one of America's great philanthropic foundations. In the face of our relatively new ability to completely destroy ourselves almost instantaneously, Dr. Hamburg called on scientists and educators everywhere to move the problem of human con-

3. Figures for universities alone are somewhat better: 61 percent have formal ties with foreign institutions and about 40 percent provide overseas experience for their faculty. See Elaine El-Khawas, *Campus Trends, 1986*, Higher Education Panel Reports, no. 73 (Washington, D.C.: American Council on Education, August 1986).

flict higher on the world's agenda. Each of us must ask ourselves "questions of practical importance," he said. "How can my organization or institution be strengthened to cope with prejudice, ethnocentrism, and hatred in a high-risk world?"[4]

Believing as I do that the universities of the world are the ideal international bridge because of our commitment to the principle of academic freedom—a commitment that goes beyond race or group loyalty, that is based on a superordinate loyalty to the freedom of the human mind to wonder and inquire—it is with alarm that I hear from Europeans of a growing nationalism in your universities and a negative attitude toward foreign students. It is with alarm that I hear of American students and their parents canceling plans for study abroad because they imagine that European universities are no longer safe, that they are caught in a backwash of terrorism. Traditionally, Americans have seen the European university as the place we go to seek our past, our common bond of Western civilization. Yet the year of study abroad has remained a serious undertaking for only a minority of American undergraduates: as of August 1986 only 18 percent of our four-year colleges and 12 percent of our universities reported that more than a tenth of their students take advantage of opportunities to study abroad.[5]

As of now the European university has its most persistent American presence in the weekly pages of the *Chronicle of Higher Education*, a newspaper read on every campus in the United States. Of approximately thirty pages a week devoted to news of higher education, the *Chronicle* allots an average of twenty-eight pages to U.S. institutions and two pages to happenings at all the rest of the colleges and universities in the world. The image which we

4. David A. Hamburg, "Prejudice, Ethnocentrism, and Violence in an Age of High Technology," reprinted from the 1984 *Annual Report* of the Carnegie Corporation of New York, p. 14.
5. El-Khawas.

receive from these reports is, as you might expect, skewed toward the bad news: that European universities are suffering from financial austerity, lack of flexibility in movement of faculty, a cumbersome system of centralized government control, pressures to adjust the curriculum to train students for available jobs, and a growing tendency toward mass higher education, ready or not.

In other words, our image of the European university is the inevitable result of selection by the news media, a spotty pattern of international collaboration, a too-thin stream of students studying abroad, and our own preoccupation with ourselves. This somewhat gloomy image is rendered awkward as well by our awareness in the United States that since World War II we have been the beneficiaries of some of the finest minds trained in European universities, the so-called brain drain, for which we gladly acknowledge our debt even as we realize the painful cost to Europe.

Obviously, if we are to do any good for each other and the world, if we are to do our share to "cope with prejudice, ethnocentrism, and hatred," we must begin with the practical recognition that we face similar problems and can offer each other valuable fruits of experience. Social scientists have postulated that the notion of education got abroad when human beings realized that each generation did not have time to learn everything by their own direct experience—at least, not if the species wanted to survive. So perhaps I could take a step in the cause of greater species longevity today by describing in very general ways the American response to some of the issues which both our systems of higher education face.

For example, you in Europe appear to be approaching common ground with us as you matriculate greater percentages of your populations and move toward a mass-education orientation. Historically, American higher education has developed according to certain generally held assumptions, such as that it is our public duty to educate all who desire it and that the correct attitude toward central government control of education is one of suspicion. These democratic assumptions have resulted in a tradition of lay control of both our public and private sectors and financial reliance on private philanthropy and state, rather than direct federal, funding.

Today in the United States a widely diverse system of higher education serves a student population of well over twelve million, nearly 60 percent of whom attend school full time. Our two-year technical institutes and community colleges grant associate degrees which permit students to enter the work force in skilled trades or to continue at a four-year college. This part of the system was developed in the 1960s to provide geographic accessibility to higher education for every citizen, to meet the needs of business and industry in particular regions, and to serve a college preparatory function for less-advantaged members of the population. We also have a large number of four-year liberal arts colleges which grant bachelor's degrees; a smaller number of specialized institutions such as conservatories and other professional schools; and an extensive system of comprehensive, graduate degree-granting and doctoral institutions, approximately 100 of which can be classified as major research universities.

Some of these schools are fully residential, some are not; some have campuses which provide them with separate space apart from the community, others are fully integrated into their urban landscapes and include a large number of commuting and night students. Whatever their size or location, the number and variety of these schools have been a response through the years to the immediate needs of American society. Thus in 1984, 33.2 percent of our high school graduates were pursuing postsecondary education at some level, and places were readily available for all of them.[6] Additionally, the low-cost, high quality education that

6. U.S. Bureau of the Census, *Statistical Abstract of the United States: 1986*, 106th ed. (Washington, D.C.: U.S. Government Printing Office, 1985), p. 149.

is available in our public-sector universities guarantees first-rate training for all of those graduates who are academically gifted.

In this way we have not compromised the quality or integrity of our highest-level educational institutions, the top tier of fifty-six major research universities which comprise the American Association of Universities, of which my own institution, Duke, is one. In both our public and private sectors, major doctoral-granting universities share the same basic mission and characteristics: the commitment to research and the resources necessary to support it; the commitment to maintaining a distinguished faculty, as determined by their peers; and most important, the commitment to academic values, which we might define simply as that system of principle and conduct which best supports the discovery of truth and its transfer to succeeding generations.

This split in American higher education between public and private schools has produced two equally strong sectors because both are well financed and self-governing. When I speak of the public sector of higher education, I am referring to our state university systems as opposed to privately endowed colleges and universities such as Duke. Although in the United States we have a federal secretary of education, neither his nor any other department of the federal government has direct control over higher education in either sector. In the state systems the legislatures and state boards have a diffuse governing role based on the power to legislate money and the political mandate to serve the broadest possible public interest. Thus, although they are large, these public systems respond to the immediate needs of their regions quickly and specifically without disturbing the academic freedom of their faculties. In my own state of North Carolina, for example, the people of the state at various times have perceived the need for more medical doctors in the eastern section, for better veterinary medicine to serve our agricultural industry, and for a professional conservatory of the arts that our young people could afford to attend. Thus the state legislature provided for our citizens' medical, economic, and artistic needs by establishing new schools, but once established, each of these schools runs its own academic affairs within the stated mission of the law which created it.

A complex of funding sources for both of these sectors further protects our autonomy and thereby our academic freedom. Our public colleges and universities are primarily, though not exclusively, supported by state monies. Our private colleges and universities are chiefly supported by private philanthropy and tuition income, although we receive a significant amount of state and federal government support through student aid and research grants. The most obvious financial mark of difference between the public and the private university is student tuition, which is quite low in the public sector, allowing these schools to fulfill their mandate to perform the broadest possible mission of public service. Incidentally, this points up the complementarity of our dual system: nearly 85 percent of specialized institutions in the United States, such as theological schools, medical schools, schools of art, music, and design, are to be found in the private sector.

The voluntary giving category of donor support for higher education in the United States can perhaps give the best idea of the flexibility built into the system. At a publicly supported institution, roughly 5 to 6 percent of expenditures come from voluntary giving sources such as alumni, corporations, and foundations. Such a percentage provides the institution with academic maneuvering room and affords individuals an opportunity to make crucial contributions in selected areas. At a private university such as Duke, voluntary giving sources provide about 20 percent of the expense budget. We also draw on endowment income (10 to 11 percent), student tuition (29 percent), and large federal government research grants. But with these going primarily to our medical center, the arts and sciences campus of the university is insulated from direct federal pressures. Fundraising is a major preoccupation at colleges and universities in the United

States because their survival depends on it. Last year foundations gave almost $1.2 billion to colleges and universities; alumni gave $1.46 billion; and corporations gave $1.57 billion, which was 25 percent of the total voluntary support to higher education in 1984–85. Last year was the first in which corporate donations exceeded gifts from alumni and foundations. These corporate donations included philanthropic gifts of cash and equipment as well as grants in support of sponsored research.[7]

This voluntary giving above and beyond the percent of an American's tax dollar that goes to higher education constitutes the additional funding of a public trust and an assumption about the future: that it can and will be affected by our efforts in the classroom and the research laboratory, and in accordance with high principles. For despite complex demands, we have maintained our credibility with the American people by safeguarding freedom of academic inquiry while we work for solutions to immediate and taxing problems. This is by no means easy, of course, and the relationship of the American university with American industry is a case in point.

Philanthropic giving to higher education by corporations is higher than it has ever been and represents a relatively uncomplicated relationship. We ascribe to these corporate dollars straightforward motives of responsible citizenship and the natural desire of American business to be known for responsible citizenship; and, like other voluntary gifts, this money and equipment come with no hidden clauses affecting academic freedom. But the university-industry research relationship is a different matter, for it promises not only rewards to the university, to industry, and to society, but also dangers to traditional academic values and to

7. Council for Financial Aid to Education, Council for Advancement and Support of Education, National Association of Independent Schools, *Voluntary Support of Education 1984–1985* (New York: CFAE, May 1986), pp. 3, 4.

the esteem in which the university is held by the public which supports it and by the faculty who comprise it. The motives of industry and the university in regard to research are, of course, in potential conflict. The profit incentive motivates industry to look for immediate commercial application of research results. The faculty of a university, on the other hand, believe that the search for truth is its own reward and that knowledge resulting from that search is to be disseminated for the public good.

But material benefits derived from long-term university research flowing more quickly out to the public and inward to the university and the faculty can play a legitimate if guarded role in keeping the university freestanding and strong.

In spite of cutbacks the federal government still funds the vast majority of research at American universities and is likely to continue to do so. But the knowledge explosion in areas such as biotechnology and microelectronics has made the academic research lab more attractive to industry than ever before, while the possibilities for patentable inventions and the hope of substantial royalty income has increased the willingness of American universities to look at relationships with industry. Given the growing financial dependence of American universities on corporations, it is appropriate to share our experience of this corporate-academic interface with you as you contemplate a growing rapprochement with industry. Recent studies at the Harvard University Center for Health Policy have focused on the relationships between industry and biotechnology faculty members at some forty major U.S. universities in departments of biochemistry, molecular biology, genetics, microbiology, biology, cellular biology, and botany. Many findings were quite positive: faculty members doing industry-sponsored research reported more publications and professional activity than their peers, with no concomitant diminution in teaching involvement. In addition, some 60 percent of these faculty members said they believe industry support of research enhances career opportunities for their students. It also increased the earnings of these faculty members, a plus for universities during difficult economic times.[8]

The risks in these relationships also surfaced, however. When queried about the extent to which possible commercial application of their research influenced their choice of topic, faculty supported in their research by industry were four times more likely to say that they had been influenced than were their colleagues. Furthermore, 70 percent of these faculty members agreed that university-industry research relationships "pose the risk of shifting too much emphasis to applied research."[9]

Perhaps the greatest concern we all have about these relationships, I think you will agree, is whether industry is likely to interfere with the free flow of ideas among colleagues and the commitment of the university to rapid sharing of new knowledge for the public good.

The Harvard findings suggest that there is cause for considerable concern. The question was posed, "Have you personally conducted any research at your university the results of which are the property of the sponsor and cannot be published without their consent?" The reply is startling. Faculty at more than half of the universities in the sample replied yes and identified industry as their research sponsor.[10]

In general, American universities are just beginning to deal with the implications of research relationships with industry. Notable among those who have are Stanford, Harvard, MIT, Yale, and Duke. Our faculty are involved in industry-sponsored research and recently developed a policy governing these relationships which we have adopted. It is typical of policies at most of

8. David Blumenthal et al., "University-Industry Research Relationships in Biotechnology: Implications for the University," *Science* 232 (June 13, 1986), 1361–66.

9. Blumenthal, p. 1364.

10. Blumenthal, p. 1364.

the AAU institutions and identifies eight areas of potential concern and specific guidelines for resolving them.

First, to protect the faculty's control over their professional work, no principal investigator can be required, as a condition of employment, "to participate in a particular research effort"; and second, if faculty choose to do sponsored research, they, and not the sponsor, "have final authority over the design and control of that research."

Third, while an industrial sponsor has the right to review papers being prepared for publication "to prevent inadvertent disclosure of . . . proprietary information," such reviews may not delay publication more than ninety days. And, in any event, final determination of what may or may not be published remains with the university.

Fourth and fifth, an industry sponsor may not restrict the freedom of faculty members to communicate with their colleagues or to take on additional sponsored work in related areas unless it can be shown to the university's satisfaction that such additional work "infringes on proprietary rights" of the first sponsor.

Sixth, while the university cannot guarantee results, we do pledge that "a good faith effort will be made to organize research projects in a manner which is sensitive to the special needs and time constraints of the sponsor."

Seventh, graduate students usually may not participate in research involving proprietary information because of the risk such a condition poses to the very basis of graduate education.

And finally, eighth, faculty members may not participate in outside activities which, by reason of the possibility of bias in the relationship or because of the amount of time and effort involved, would conflict with their obligations to the university.

Such policies are much needed, for the frame of reference in which industry and the university work, although apparently the same for both participants, is in fact quite different. Industry is concerned with keeping expenses down, with bargaining to get the most for their dollar, with getting results, and with beating their competitors to the market with a wonderful commercial idea. In addition, because universities serve the public, there is a tendency for business to view them as similar to public libraries, filled with free information waiting to be tapped. Understandably, business people want to keep their dealings in a context with which they are familiar. They bring this context with them onto the university campus and they operate from certain assumptions, valid everywhere except in this peculiar environment, where faculty members are not employees though they receive compensation for their efforts, and where making money is only a secondary reality—a means rather than an end.

These realities do clash: They clash when the university is raided for ideas and knowledge by agents who give no thought to providing for the material needs of an institution on which our very world depends. They clash when our resources are diverted to commercial purposes without advancing the mission of the university either in knowledge gained or transmitted. They clash when faculty members become enmeshed in contracts they do not fully understand. They clash when the university is held to worldly standards and values of self-interest that debase and confuse our efforts and sadden our hopes. But we are, after all, the educational institutions in these proposed partnerships, and it is for us to determine the safe conditions under which they can be undertaken, to provide the canary in the mine. By developing specific written policies to guide faculty members, the university can be protected and industry can be educated to the differences in our separate spheres and the points at which we can work fruitfully together.

Such policies also can—and should—speak to the concerns of business. As a psychiatrist I long ago appreciated the value of letting the other fellow know you understand his point of view and what his needs are even if there isn't much you can do about them. Our policy speaks to these concerns, establishing that we do not seek an adversarial relationship and acknowledging that we have different roles to play in a healthy society. And, too, it is a good opportunity to prove that we mean to stand by our principles. It is possible, after all, for a faculty member to take unfair advantage of the industrial partner in a research relationship: to hire cheap, inexperienced laboratory help, thereby diverting industry funds to other uses and damaging the project; to slow down the rate of work so as to receive funds over a longer period of time; to give only token participation in the research, thereby not delivering the expertise that had been paid for.

Certainly we believe that these things happen rarely, if at all, but we cannot guarantee that they will not. To take advantage of our resources—our faculty at the cutting edge of knowledge, our research labs already in place with trained technicians and sophisticated equipment—industry must rely on our tradition of acting in good faith for the benefit of society. It cannot hurt in developing these relationships for policy documents to suggest, however obliquely, the inherent contradiction that lies in industry exploitation of the university. For to profit from a relationship with us, industry must rely on our integrity, strengthened through centuries of keeping faith with society. To exploit the university by taking unfair advantage of that historic good faith is an irony that can only serve to poison our interactions and rebound on the deceiver.

That research relationships between the university and industry are becoming more frequent is, of course, a response to global economic conditions. The university must respond to changing societal demands even as it guards its traditional values and role. Then, having entered responsibly into these relationships, the university faces the question of proper management of any technology which arises from that research. In the case of a corporate sponsor, most universities attempt to retain the patent rights to inventions of their faculty, allowing industry to purchase an option to license any patentable technology. Return to the faculty member from any royalties on an invention is usually based on a percentage formula which divides proceeds among the principal investigator, the lab or department involved, and the university general fund, after university expenses have been paid. In the case of federally sponsored research, the American university has had considerable incentive to develop its own patenting and licensing program since the Patent Law amendments of 1980 returned to us rights on any patentable inventions resulting from federally sponsored research.

We do not as yet know if patent royalties will ever make a substantial financial return to universities. A recent study of the patenting and licensing program at the University of Wisconsin—possibly the oldest such effort in the United States—shows that in its first half century the program contributed approximately $99 million to the university's research budget. However, this amount represents only about 5 percent of the monies spent on research during those years.[11] These figures suggest that we should move ahead cautiously, weighing factors such as the expense of running professional in-house operations versus the uncertainty of significant profits, the likelihood of patent-infringement lawsuits, and the dangers of appearing to encourage faculty-industry interaction to the detriment of our traditional mission. It is tempting for those who worry about our university budgets to push us imperceptibly closer to the industrial purse—especially so when corporate executives sit on our boards of trustees and in our state legislatures and in Congress. And as the economic crunch comes, it is the faculty and its administrators who must resist converting our universities—America's and eventually yours—into corporate-driven research institutes.

In North Carolina we have sought to create a buffer zone be-

11. David Blumenthal et al., "Commercializing University Research: Lessons from the Experience of the Wisconsin Alumni Research Foundation," *New England Journal of Medicine* 314, no. 25 (June 19, 1986), p. 1623.

tween one vital sphere of activity in our society and another. The state entered into partnership with corporations and three universities to purchase six thousand acres of land. The land was then donated to a foundation which in turn leases the land to corporations seeking to site research and development laboratories in North Carolina. The foundation has now funded the three universities to set up a marketing office for patents and licenses derived from the work of our three faculties. In this way we hope to share costs, risks, and expertise as well as protect ourselves with a liaison island.

It occurs to me as we consider these things that you and I are part of one world, while business and industry are part of another, equally necessary world. I have been concentrating on an outline of the difficulties in creating liaison with that world, a situation I find much more comprehensible than the fact that close liaison among our universities has remained a mostly unfulfilled dream. We share a devotion to the life of the mind; should that allegiance not bring us closer together, across geographic and political boundaries? Yes, you are thinking, it is easy to make rhetorical statements, much harder to follow them with practical suggestions and action. I agree. And the blueprints for action must come from the individual institutions according to their responsibilities and needs. But I can make a few specific suggestions; and I do say to you that the AAU institutions are ready and eager to follow up on these and others with specific action that will meet our mutual needs. For we must eliminate estrangement among the universities of the world.

We would ask you to be more flexible in the matter of academic exchange of our faculty and students. We need to work out methods for transfer of academic credit so that our graduate students can spend a year abroad at parity; and our faculty need the option of varying the periods of time during which they would agree to teach abroad. We would also be interested in working out with you a method for international transfer of technology developed at our universities, in formulating a way to overcome the intricacies of international licensing agreements. And it seems to me that one of the most exciting possibilities waiting for us is the computerized hook-up of our libraries; mutual access to the databanks of American and European universities is not an impossible dream.

You probably realize that many American universities utilize computer software for a variety of administrative purposes, including accounting packages that could help you in calculating research as opposed to teaching costs, and software developed for our hospital patient care system which is currently being used in European hospitals. We have tools and knowledge to share with you, and we have much to learn and a growing desire to bring greater unity to the academic world—a desire that we ask you to match for the sake of the larger society for which we hold so much in trust.

I would close by suggesting to you that barriers between us may be less nationalistic than they are psychological. Let me offer a parable from contemporary literature.

One of last year's most popular American novels was a book called *The Accidental Tourist* by Anne Tyler. Its protagonist was a man who hated to travel and who made his living by writing guidebooks to the major cities of the world. These guidebooks sold very well indeed because this man who hated to leave home specialized in scouting out bits of America in every European capital. Thus, the American purchaser of his guides could travel across international boundaries and ignore the reality of his outward circumstances by doggedly eating at American fast food restaurants no matter where he went. And so the American comforted and reassured himself with the familiar and avoided becoming any more than accidentally a tourist in another land.

The Accidental Tourist is a very funny book because it only slightly exaggerates an all too prevalent American attitude of insularity, an attitude I fear is present among the citizens of every country. Like the accidental tourist, we are all guilty of a failure to take account of the rest of the world. We encounter one another across international boundaries, if not accidentally, then at the very most tentatively, hesitant travelers, obstinate, unsure, uncomfortable.

I have not come to Madrid as an accidental tourist. I have come to observe, to learn, and to join you in substantive discussion to find ways of bringing our institutions closer together. Let us pledge ourselves and our universities to the role of academic *agents provocateurs*, in the hope that we can incite the whole world to a less narrow, fearful, and more liable humanity.

In Defense of Professors

*"Paradise Tossed: The Fall of Literary Standards" (*Washington Post*), "From Western Lit to Westerns as Lit" (*Wall Street Journal*), "Barbaric Betrayal" (*San Diego Union*)—in the early months of 1988, Duke was taking hits in the national press from coast to coast for an English department that was supposedly "trashing" the classics to make room for Louis L'Amour,* The Color Purple, *and works by women, non-Western, and minority authors. In fact, under newly appointed chair Stanley Fish, both the English department and the study of the classics were thriving at Duke as our scholars went about their proper business: thinking about, writing about, and exploring with their students the meaning and uses of literature and art in contemporary civilization.*

On June 5 the New York Times Magazine*'s cover story, "The Battle of the Books," featured Duke English department faculty in a rare balanced account of the controversy. And in September, in response to continuing attacks on liberal arts faculties in the press and by high-level officials in the U.S. Department of Education and the National Endowment for the Humanities, Duke and the University of North Carolina at Chapel Hill sponsored a conference where scholars and the public could come together to discuss the issues without the kind of overstatement, misstatement, or disinformation that had characterized debate over the literary canon up to then.*

OPENING REMARKS
DUKE–UNIVERSITY OF NORTH CAROLINA CONFERENCE ON LIBERAL ARTS EDUCATION IN THE LATE TWENTIETH CENTURY
SEPTEMBER 16, 1988

I would like to add to Paul's [Paul Hardin, chancellor of the University of North Carolina at Chapel Hill] welcome to this extraordinary collaborative undertaking by the faculty of our two universities a word or two in defense of our university faculties everywhere.

It is certainly unusual when academics grab headlines for thinking about literature.

It is undoubtedly rare for professors to gain national attention because of what they put on their reading lists and what they say in their classrooms.

Seldom have I known impassioned editorials and commentaries in the media to be inspired by so unassuming a thing as a course syllabus.

Yet such has been the case in recent months, as faculty not only at Duke but at a number of other universities have grabbed those headlines, gained that attention, and in many instances been not just reported on, but pilloried for the sake of a syllabus. It would appear that at long last the liberal arts have achieved a level of notoriety usually reserved for university athletic departments. I, for one, devoutly hope that the humanities professors on our campuses might also gain someday a level of support, of celebration, and of percipient analysis similar to that accorded basketball and football teams. To date, however, misunderstanding, oversimplification, even vilification have been the order of the day for faculty members at distinguished institutions all over the country.

In this context I am irresistibly reminded of a succinct comment by the creator of detective hero Travis McGee, the late John D. MacDonald. "To be aware of the world [we] live in," he writes, we must be able to comprehend, "complex ideas and complex relationships"—ideas and relationships that cannot be "transmitted by body language . . . brainstorming sessions . . . the boob tube or the boom box."[1] Nor, might I add, by news nuggets, irresponsible rhetoric, or even "in-depth" reporting. In the past quarter of a century our nation and our world have become increasingly complex economically and demographically, through science and technology.

We think we have made great progress. Today an estimated 27 million adult Americans cannot read and write;[2] in Asia, Africa, and Latin America some 500 million people are slowly starving to death;[3] there's a hole in the ozone layer over Antarctica; the rain forests are disappearing but man's inhumanity to man is not. Obviously, how we teach our brightest young people to think about our world is important. Obviously, how we think about our world is a matter of survival and so are the tools of knowledge and understanding that we bring to the struggle. Suddenly, we have opened our eyes. Suddenly, reading lists have taken on a whole new meaning as we realize the implications of our so-called progress and of the millions of human beings all over the world who have been left behind and who are not—who must not be regarded as—expendable.

Enter the disruptive spirits of the liberal arts faculties, who know that the search for knowledge and truth has implications, has responsibilities, bears the burden of interpreting the human costs and the human realities of our advances. Now, we all agree that human civilization requires human contexts and values—contexts and values derived from history and literature, from the study of the philosophies and religions, the languages and cul-

1. John D. MacDonald, *Reading for Survival* (Washington, D.C.: Center for the Book in the Library of Congress, 1987), pp. 24–25.

2. Lee A. Daniels, "Illiteracy Seen as Threat to U.S. Economic Edge," *New York Times*, Sept. 7, 1988, sec. 1, p. 23, col. 3.

3. "The Causes of Hunger," *Seeds* 11, no. 8 (Aug. 1988), 18.

tures of the world—and it is here, perhaps, that the disagreements start, for it is the world that we are dealing with these days, not just the neighborhood. The provision of this context is a strenuous mandate, even a moral charge that we, as a society, have laid on our college faculties. And we are well served—best served—by those faculty who have never accepted and never believed that providing a liberal education is the static, unmolested, and comfortable activity that those who take potshots at the "ivory tower" assume it to be.

A university is, after all, meant to be a subversive institution; is meant to overthrow entrenched attitudes of inhumanity, arrogance, and intolerance; is a place of differing people with different perspectives, lives, ideas, opinions; a place such as the great English poet John Milton described, "where there is much desire to learn . . . much arguing, much writing, many opinions; for opinion . . . is but knowledge in the making."[4]

It is especially appropriate that members of the freshman class of the UNC Honors Program are with us for today's sessions. It is around you, the students, after all, that these controversies swirl, these controversies over higher education, about what you are going to be taught and what you are going to read for the next four years. I hope you will carry away from this conference a sense of the vitality of American scholarship; of what it means to acquire an attitude of intellectual skepticism; of how it is that knowledgeable men and women of good will can disagree, and why honest disagreements are the fuel of democracy. Your professors at the University of North Carolina, our professors at Duke University, professors on liberal arts campuses all over the country are people who have devoted their lives to thinking about difficult issues and ideas that touch our world and our selves at a thousand different places. Their ideas are not amenable to simplistic and polarized interpretation any more than

4. John Milton, "Areopagitica" (1644).

are the complex realities of our late-twentieth-century world. In your classes you will find, just as at this conference, that professors are strong-minded people who can help you—who can help all of us—to understand something of the different things that there are in the world; who can introduce us to knowledge that, in the words of Gerard Manley Hopkins, gives thanks for "All things counter,/original,/ spare,/ strange."[5] And in the process of acquiring such an education, you will learn to be amazed by the common boundaries of our humanity.

And now, having quoted from a renegade Catholic priest, from a Protestant poet imprisoned for his political convictions, and from a best-selling author of detective fiction, thereby placing myself squarely in the best eclectic tradition of the liberal arts at Duke University, let me wish you a successful, a rewarding, and a thoroughly provoking conference.

5. Gerard Manley Hopkins, "Pied Beauty" (1948 [1918]).

On Collegiality

Each year I made a state of the university address as part of the annual meeting of the faculty. At first these meetings were held in Page Auditorium, but by 1988 we had changed our venue to the regular meeting place of the Academic Council in the Social Sciences Building. Here the chair of the council and I would each present our year-end reports on what Yale president Bart Giamatti once referred to as getting the university through the day[1]*—enrollment figures, budgets, program development, planning efforts, faculty recruitment, fundraising, new buildings, deferred maintenance, promises kept, promises pending, and other such elements of the academic bottom line. But even from the beginning—and with surprising regularity, as I look back on it—the facts and figures made way for comments on the role that collegiality must play in creating and sustaining a great university. One year I was able to quote Clark Kerr, president emeritus of the University of California and originator of the term "multiversity," who had just published an essay citing broad faculty participation in governing as "particularly decisive in the most academically elite research universities. . . ."*[2] *Effec-*

1. A. Bartlett Giamatti, "A Free and Ordered Space: The Real World of the University" (informal remarks at the Gannett Center for Media Studies' 5th Annual Leadership Institute, June 19, 1989), Special Report (New York: Gannett Center for Media Studies, Dec. 1989), p. 3.
2. Clark Kerr, "The New Race to Be Harvard or Berkeley or Stanford," *Change* (May/June 1991), 15.

tive faculty governance, I had reason to know, depended on working together toward common goals with mutual respect or, in other words, on collegiality.

Certainly since my own arrival at Duke in 1974, our faculty had been vigorously involved in university governance through our Academic Council, something with which as president I was not only comfortable but experienced. At Stanford I had served as chair of the Medical School Faculty Senate; at Duke, while chair of the Department of Psychiatry, I was nominated to the Academic Council and then elected to that body's executive committee (ECAC). I served first under the chairmanship of Richard Watson and then of Anne Scott, both historians. These two, my early tutors, knew the place, they knew the issues, and they knew higher education. Thus, my time on the council was wonderful preparation for the presidency in that it gave me the faculty perspective from across the whole of the university, not just the Medical School or the arts and sciences. Furthermore, it was because of my membership on ECAC that I was given the opportunity to serve on the long-range planning committee in March of 1977, eventually working with Chancellor Ken Pye to develop "Directions for Progress" (1980), the plan ultimately approved by our trustees through which we faced some tough budgetary decisions that required closing the education department and the undergraduate nursing program.

As president I attended the regular monthly meetings of the council, ready to answer questions and to take part in the discussions. An interesting thing had occurred during the Nixon library debates[3] *in 1981:*

3. In the summer of 1981 President Terry Sanford, after consulting with several Duke faculty members, went to see Richard Nixon about locating his presidential papers at Duke. Nixon, a 1937 graduate of the Duke Law School, was positive about the suggestion, but the proposal subsequently met with stiff opposition among the Duke faculty and bitter debate in the Academic Council. On October 29, 1981, the council finally did vote to accept the papers (53 for, 0 against, 1 abstention), but rejected the museum that usually forms a part of presidential libraries. Neither Terry Sanford nor Richard Nixon chose to pursue the matter further.

the faculty had taken the vote away from the provost and the president, both of whom were, up until that time, ex officio voting members of the council. And so I was the first Duke president to come into office with no Academic Council vote. But this was fine because the Academic Council is an advice-giving body to the president, and it seemed to make little sense for the president to have a vote in giving advice to himself. The lack of a vote, however, did not prevent me from lobbying and speaking out on important issues, though for the most part I felt my role in meetings was to listen and to respond or designate other officers to respond to faculty queries.

Thus, with faculty fully involved in governance through both the standing and ad hoc committees of the Academic Council and through constant updates from members of the administration in council meetings, the issue of being able to work together effectively toward common goals was an ever present concern. Looking back, I find that I commented on collegiality at greater or lesser length in seven out of eight of my annual addresses to the faculty. In fact, as the faculty became embroiled in heated debates centering on issues of "political correctness"—altering the curriculum to reflect minority points of view or subject matter, increasing the number of black faculty and graduate students, forming a chapter of the conservative National Association of Scholars—timely remarks of self-definition, reaffirmation, and an occasional mild scolding became increasingly relevant.

ADDRESS TO THE DUKE UNIVERSITY FACULTY
DECEMBER 7, 1989

By tradition, this annual address to the faculty provides you with the president's assessment of the state of the university, replete with facts and figures and expressions of appreciation to some of the dramatis personae of the past year's achievements. But this year I depart from tradition, though I hasten to add that I am no less aware of the contributions of the many members of Duke's faculty and staff whose hard work has located solutions and negotiated agreements, and the facts and figures can be marshaled when need be to show that the university is in good shape. But this year, rather than bombard you with statistics and details, many of which you already know from the minutes of past Academic Council meetings, it seemed to me the time had come to assess with somewhat larger strokes where we are as an institution, to reaffirm our ideals, and to do this from the unique vantage point of the presidency which, so long as I serve in that office, commits me to viewing every school, department, initiative, and decision as part of a whole—a faculty-centered, academic enterprise that is one university.

When I came to this office four and a half years ago, I brought eight years of experience at the Medical School, three years as chancellor of the university, and one year as acting provost, so that I had a fund of knowledge already about Duke to bring to the presidency. But I didn't know nearly enough about the undergraduate programs or about some of the professional schools. I spent time working with the deans and the provost toward an understanding of the various academic issues, and I began teaching undergraduate seminars which keep me in the educational trenches of the college. I have learned that the problems we face at Duke are the generalized afflictions that all universities are heir to these days; it is only the details of our solutions that will be unique to us.

The generalized afflictions, the threats to universities, are many; you can list them as well and as rapidly as I, and if we should happen to leave anything out, the *Chronicle of Higher Education* will obligingly remind us every couple of weeks and provide reassurances that we are not alone: everybody's buildings are crumbling; everybody's scrambling for better salaries and more resources and the best students and outstanding faculty, while everywhere the pools are dwindling; everybody's being accused of poor teaching or not teaching, of costing too much, of not creating on campus a safer, more just and open society than the one that surrounds us.

Lately it has been my responsibility to lead us in responding to issues such as these; and I have had to guide me, in addition to outspoken and knowledgeable colleagues, some rules, or perhaps I should say principles, as a test for any decision or direction we take. These are (1) that the academic mission, as embodied in the faculty, is central; (2) that all other functions should be organized so as to strengthen that mission; and (3) that this is one university.

The nuts and bolts of addressing these issues at Duke we have discussed and reported to each other regularly, and I believe that the decisions that have been made meet the tests of these principles and the corollary of educational economy: that everything shall ultimately contribute to serving the whole, both now and in the future. The faculty-initiated commitment of Duke to interdisciplinary studies, for example, meets this test; by deciding to pursue excellence in interdisciplinary research, we strengthen portions of many individual departments, improve undergraduate education at the same time that we place our graduate students in the forefront of research, bring faculty together for fruitful collaboration, share expensive resources, and provide an exciting intellectual arena that will attract, nurture, and hold outstanding scholars. The Science Resource Initiative [the Levine Science Research Center], a response to a basic, critical need for space on our campus for the sciences, will do all of these things, serve a multitude of purposes, as all of our solutions must. Another such example is Project Nexus, an expensive and critical project now underway that will address campus-wide computer needs and support research efforts that cross the boundaries of disciplines and buildings.

We have responded judiciously—dare I say wholistically?—to other needs: new buildings are planned where necessary or most economical. In addition to the SRI we have prepared the way for a Law School wing, a building for the Institute of Policy Sciences, a new art museum, a science library complex, and a Divinity School wing, among others. Older space is in line for renovation where that is more practical, for example, the renovations planned for the Carr Building and the current art museum, where we will house the Department of Art and Art History. Most of these efforts to improve our facilities will be funded with new dollars, money to come from the Campaign for Duke.

If we haven't managed to wave a magic wand over faculty salaries, we have been able to remain competitive, moving from fourteenth to ninth among the twenty-three institutions with which we compare ourselves. In the face of changing demographics we have diversified the student body through aggressive recruiting and increased financial aid—in 1985 18 percent of our students were on need-based financial aid; now that figure is over 40 percent. Our efforts to ensure the advancement of minorities at Duke both in the faculty and the student body are firmly underway, as you are well aware, and promise that the university in future years will be enriched and our society strengthened by our actions of today.

Duke has needed to increase endowment in order to meet the costs of its ambitions: since I became president our endowment has doubled. I believe we can meet both the arts and sciences campaign goal of $200 million and the university-wide $400 million goal which will aid all segments of the university in fundraising for programs and for bricks and mortar. I hope to see this campaign through to a successful completion before returning to full-time faculty status.

In the late seventies Duke went through a retrenchment effort, and there were casualties. I do not foresee further episodes of severe retrenchment at Duke, but we have realized that we must make careful choices, choices that support excellence—those things that we can do extremely well—and we must continue to reach informed agreement about those choices together. The Academic Council's Task Force on University Governance effectively strengthened the faculty voice in decision making by providing clearer channels, and the resulting resources committee provides faculty with a very visible opportunity not only to advise on questions of allocating resources, but also to develop stronger understanding of administrative workings. We are all in this together; we all want this institution to succeed, and the faculty voice is critical in charting the course.

In the company of other private research universities, Duke faces a difficult future, but we face it with enormous vitality. As president it has been my responsibility—indeed, my privilege—to see the university whole, to referee its competing constituencies, and to attempt to keep its various parts in balance. I know the measure of its energy and the difficulty of pulling those energies back toward the center. In fact, my earliest and most sustained efforts since becoming president have been directed toward maintaining the integrity of this institution as a university—as a coherent entity that exists above and in addition to the sum of its parts.

I think we agree, for example, that a medical complex next door to an academic complex with the same name does not automatically create a university, nor is a cluster of strong professional schools loosely affiliated with an undergraduate college quite what we mean by a university either. A university has to have something to do with being conjugal, in law and in spirit. Many of the problems we face, problems of resources and conflicting purposes and needs, combine to produce centrifugal forces that interfere with this conjoining, that tend to pull research universities apart into conglomerates of separate camps, undermining both the sense and the reality of academic community. Inflation; the escalating price tag on modern science; and the unfamiliar, competitive nature of the new academic marketplace have created obvious inequities in salaries and resources. The sheer numbers of faculty mean that hundreds of colleagues are strangers to one another. The twin demands of research and teaching can shift after a decade or more from creative tension to imbalance and even burnout on one side of the equation or the other. And the complexities and the time required to manage the affairs of the multiple constituencies that make up the research university leave many faculty frustrated and disenchanted with the governance process. Increasingly one hears of faculty who feel a greater sense of fellowship and community within their own discipline than within their own university.

The current strains on collegiality and the price we all pay for those strains are not trivial. You may have read the results of a recent faculty survey reported in the *Chronicle of Higher Education.* Some 72 percent of the faculty at research universities consider their administration to be autocratic. Two-thirds think that their institution is managed ineffectively. Sixty percent find that there has been a widespread lowering of standards, and one-half admit that their jobs are a source of considerable personal strain. Only 45 percent perceive their own salaries as good or excellent.[4]

One would hope that a similar survey at Duke would yield more positive results, but there is no denying that we also partake of the malaise that the complexities of large research universities produce: Duke's employment total of 17,000 and its budget of over $900 million can't help but provoke the uneasy sensation that a corporate monstrosity is breathing down the backs of our collective academic necks. In the sciences, faculty are caught in the ceaseless pursuit of outside grants, the intricacies of federal policy, and the ambiguities of industry-sponsored research, while in the liberal arts, the law of supply and demand has caused an unprecedented salary explosion of superstars and superfields that leaves the majority of faculty behind.

Outside critics and even sympathetic observers seldom remark

4. Carolyn J. Mooney, "Carnegie Faculty Survey: Professors Are Upbeat about Profession but Uneasy about Students, Standards," *Chronicle of Higher Education*, Nov. 8, 1989, A21.

on the breakdown of collegiality as one of the threats to universities. But within the academy we know that the alienation of scholars from each other and from their home institutions is one of the greatest threats to the university as we understand it, because the university *is* the faculty. Robert Maynard Hutchins, who had the pleasure of leading Chicago back in the good old days when university presidents were infamous for their educational ideas rather than their athletic departments, provides us with a definition of the university which I like because it is short and more than just a little bit bad tempered. "A university," he writes, "is a community of scholars. It is not a kindergarten; it is not a club; it is not a reform school; it is not a political party; it is not an agency of propaganda. A university is a community of scholars."[5]

Whether this is a definition or an outburst I cannot say, but it makes the point. We are a community of scholars bound by shared ideas, values, and goals. And for some reason, despite our differences, we have traditionally believed and continue to suspect that there is something to be gained by staying together—linguists and engineers, historians and scientists, mathematicians and artists, those who have to do with literature and those who have to do with lasers. Another way of saying it is that even on our worst days we have a hunch that something would be lost by going our separate ways. And what that something lost would be is our share of the covenant that the university has made with society, that here will be ground set aside, protected, to comprise a varied fellowship of those who are to teach and to think independently and without fear of reprisal and for something even more compelling than money—for the chance at discovery.

We need this fellowship, this collegiality—we need each other. Otherwise there is no community of scholars—no sharing of knowledge or mores, no mentoring, no honorable and selfless

5. Robert Maynard Hutchins, "What Is a University?" (radio address, April 18, 1935), in *No Friendly Voice* (Chicago: University of Chicago Press, 1936), p. 5.

teaching, no care for the future, and worse: no freedom of inquiry, no independent thought, no iconoclastic thought, no abnormal, unprofitable, offensive thought; in the words of the poet, no long, long thoughts. In short, no university.

And so we have to believe that beyond quarrels and wrongs and inequities and mistakes, there is ultimately something to be served here, something that enlarges, lengthens, connects our individual contributions to our society and to the future. For better or worse, we are faculty married to an enterprise worth preserving.

Higher Education and the Competitive Edge

If the decade of the eighties was the era of the poll in presidential politics, it was also the decade when institutional research moved out of the stodgy pages of education journals and the realm of higher education professionals into the more glamorous purview of journalism and the dubious rewards of fame and amateur assessment. Since 1983 the best known of the college rankings has been U.S. News and World Report*'s "America's Best Colleges" issue, with which many of my fellow presidents and I have had an ambivalent relationship. Because we are familiar with scholarly analyses of institutional quality (such as the National Research Council rankings) which assess the relative merits of university programs of study by polling faculty in their own fields, the flaws in the oversimplified* U.S. News *surveys are, to our eyes, glaring. The methodology for the surveys has varied from year to year, making comparisons difficult; criteria combine objective data with subjective evaluations from a variety of college administrators; and the magazine prominently describes its rankings as based on an "exclusive," "nationwide survey of college presidents," thus lending a validity to the ratings with which many of us are far from comfortable. One of the implications is, of course, that participation equals endorsement. Another is that college presidents,* ex officio, *are automatically experts on every other college or university in the country.*

In 1989, seeing that the presidents' responses would eventually count for 25 percent of each college's final ranking, I sent a letter to the editor of U.S. News and World Report *in lieu of the questionnaire: "It has be-*

come increasingly clear to me that university presidents are probably the least knowledgeable to comment on the quality of an undergraduate education in competing institutions. I fear that the results of such a survey can be misleading for students and parents alike." The following year I again wrote a letter to the editor, saying in part, "I do not believe university presidents are in a position to know enough to intelligently respond to the survey you have prepared. We know our own universities well, and a few others with which we compare ourselves, but to do justice to the many institutions you have asked us to rank is, for me, impossible."

This time I received a cordial and lengthy response from the editor:

> *How can the absence of knowledge be relevant to a survey that proposes to evaluate colleges and universities on the basis of the best and latest information? . . . Rightly or wrongly, the brand names of higher education, regardless of their actual quality, carry more weight with the corporate personnel officer or professional school admissions dean than do the institutions about which they, like you, "know very little." . . . as long as the name "Duke" on a diploma gains the entree for its graduates that it does among people who do not know an SAT score from a golf score, I believe we should keep trying to measure reputation. And although it is sometimes decried as a "beauty contest," our annual reputational survey is one of the few sources for information about how those best positioned to make judgments about academic reputations perceive their peers. In effect, we are asking college officials to become surrogates for the corporate and professional school recruiters that their graduates someday will face.*
>
> *To sum up: our reputational survey which accounts for 25 per cent of any college's overall rating in the* U.S. News *study seeks to measure perceptions because perceptions are often more important than reality.*

While the cynicism expressed in the editor's reply is no doubt appropriate to journalism and the marketplace, it seems to me a futile yardstick by which to measure the quality of an education.

The questions raised by the U.S. News *rankings continued to trouble me, and when I was asked to address a conference of secondary school educators on their meeting's theme, "Competition: A Tool for Learning," I saw an opportunity to revisit the controversy and some of its broader implications.*

ADDRESS TO THE COUNTRY DAY SCHOOL HEADMASTERS' ASSOCIATION JUNE 21, 1990

My role is usually to welcome distinguished visitors to Duke and share in the joy of anticipation. Tonight, however, I am pleased to be your send-off speaker, to ponder with you the theme of your 1990 conference in the context of my experience with a research university.

I imagine it has not been unusual lately for the parents of your college-bound juniors and seniors to ask for comments and advice in regard to the current public questions about—and in some instances, attacks on—our colleges and universities. In fact, your request for remarks related to this meeting's concerns led me to realize just how closely intertwined with issues of competition most of these criticisms really are. You can list the issues as readily as I: intercollegiate athletics; the bidding for "superstar" professors; questions of collusion on financial aid packages; unseemly rivalry for the top 5 or 10 percent of high school students; competition over tuition hikes, fundraising, government contracts—we could go on all evening. So, I will save time and concede: American higher education is a chip off the old capitalist block, the true and natural child of a highly successful, competitive society. Our universities have been built on the fruits of a vigorous marketplace and they operate by many of its rules and concepts, with the result that higher education in this country is acknowledged to be the very best in the world.

But having said this much, wisdom directs that I leave the

heady garden of self-congratulation for the thornier grounds of old human nature. I am sure it doesn't surprise you that as a physician and a psychiatrist, I tend to think in images of health and of disease and to see in many examples of human behavior the perversion of natural instincts—the debasing, if you will, of what is good and fruitful for human life into instruments of sterility and even destructiveness. In your conference this week you have been considering the merits and properties of competition as an educational tool. My own education and training have taught me that the competitive spirit in human beings is the natural psychological component of biologically determined aggression, one of our species' most important tools for survival. Yet we know how quickly this necessary aggressive drive in human beings to subdue their environment and protect their young can be turned to unnecessary hostility and violence—unnecessary in the context of an established civilization, when physical aggression within the human community becomes a perversion of otherwise beneficial competitive drives.

This concept of a perversion of competition I have found it interesting to apply to more sophisticated levels of social functioning. For example, we have noted that America's higher education is the best in the world as a result of sustained national prosperity and the competition among institutions for the best faculty, the best students, the best teaching facilities, the greatest amount of government funding, and so on. Yet somehow, in this national competitive heat, we have failed to protect our young, we have failed to guard their learning environment against the depredations of hostile social forces, with the result that we are now charged with having one of the worst systems of public primary and secondary education in the world. Among 158 United Nations member nations, the United States ranks forty-ninth in literacy; 40 percent of our armed services enlistees read below the ninth grade level; and last year a National Research Council report concluded that most U.S. students leave school with math skills too poor to perform most jobs.[1] A sorry showing in any event, but particularly accusatory in the face of our sparkling record elsewhere.

We can find another perverse outcome in our health care system. America's competition-driven economy has produced the most lavishly equipped research laboratories, the largest supply of scientists, the most advanced medical technology, the best trained physicians, and the biggest state-of-the-art hospitals in the world. There is no better medical care anywhere—if you or the organization you work for can afford it. Professionals call our system "two-tier medical care," meaning that some thirty-five million Americans with little or no medical insurance are on the bottom rung, receiving poorly administered, patched together, haphazard services. And while the rest of us are situated comfortably at the top, the U.S. infant mortality rate, shamefully, ranks twenty-second in the world.[2] Truly, this is a perverse product of the competition that has created so much wealth, knowledge, and expertise for our nation.

If we turn to business, we can reference the leveraged buyouts and hostile takeovers that produce nothing—no new products, no additional jobs, no healthy new industry—just incredible increases in the cost of doing business. We see the phenomenon of sterile greed, the perversion of a healthy human drive to achieve. Sadly, at times turning to the business section of the newspaper is like signing up for a tour with the seven deadly sins, as the Boeskys and the Milkens and the S&L managers[3] perform their

1. Democratic Policy Committee, *Education Accomplishments 1990*, Special Report no. 21 (Washington, D.C.: U.S. Senate, Feb. 8, 1990), pp. 4, 9.

2. U.S. Department of Health and Human Services, *Health United States 1989* (Hyattsville, M.D.: March 1990), p. 11.

3. Ivan Boesky was convicted of insider trading in 1986, fined $100 million, and served two years of a three-year prison sentence. "Junk-bond king" Michael Milken was convicted in 1990 for multiple violations of the Securities and Exchange Act, paid a $600 million fine, and served less than two years of a ten-

own renditions of pride, avarice, envy, gluttony, lust, anger, and a new twist on sloth: the philosophy that actually manufacturing something or building up a new company is just too much work, especially when you can get so much more for yourself by corporate raiding—gobbling up the cash and other assets of the victim of a leveraged buyout, shutting down the research-and-development function for the future, and milking the company for a few years until it goes under. It is sad to see the giants fall, victims of the leveraged buyout—a perversion of the goals of healthy competition.

Let us return now to higher education, where we can see that our society has created a fleet of extraordinary institutions that sail in the eye of the hurricane—at the very center of a cyclone of competing forces. Take, for example, my own institution. As a research university Duke is a typically American invention. It is expected to be all things educational that a society could need: to educate young adults in the professions and to educate late adolescents in the liberal arts; to disseminate knowledge, but also to discover and create it; to perform an essential public service, but to beg, borrow, and charge tuition to pay for most of these services ourselves (a condition that holds true more and more for public universities as well). We have promised society that we will provide "ivory towers" to shelter and nurture over the long term the intellectual and creative elite who constitute our national "think tank." Yet we must be prepared to respond like an institutional minuteman to our hard-pressed country's most immediate real world needs, whether technological or ecological, economic or political, military or medical.

The university's competing responsibilities today seem over-

---

year prison sentence. Deregulation of the savings and loan industry in the early 1980s permitted the risky and unethical practices by S&L owners, managers, and directors that caused hundreds of institutions to require federal bailouts in excess of $80 billion by 1992 and still mounting.

whelming. Duke is a not-for-profit institution that nevertheless pays a workforce of 18,000, making it the single largest private employer in North Carolina. Thus, we must be responsive to the interests of those who work here as well as to those who come here to learn. We have fiduciary responsibilities for the philanthropic funds entrusted to us, we have moral responsibilities for the young lives we powerfully influence, we have ethical responsibilities for the dissemination and use of the knowledge we discover here. We might even be said to bear a sort of guild responsibility as guardians of this peculiar idea of a university as Americans have created it to serve the even more peculiar American idea of a government—an idea about intellectual freedom, about the absolute value of education to the conduct of a democracy, about the faith that by putting massive resources into the strange and paradoxical collection that is the university, an enlightened society will find answers to its most pressing problems.

Our assignment, then—higher education's assignment—is to keep all the plates spinning, all the balls in the air; and competition is the element constantly forcing the juggler's hand. The strain this creates leads to frequent confusion on the part of the public and contention within the academy, contention fueled by fear that the scholarship and teaching missions of the university will become subverted and eclipsed. This fear is not unrealistic. As you very well know, in the years since the Second World War, American universities have accumulated more and more power, greater and greater resources, and consequently have become well acquainted with the natural offspring of power and resources: vaulting ambition and the competitive pressures that drive those ambitions.

Perhaps nothing crystallizes better the ambivalence the university community feels in this matter of competitiveness than the yearly ratings of "America's Best Colleges" in *U.S. News and World Report*. Certainly, it is great fun to be labeled a "winner" in a national magazine with a readership of some two and a half million; after all, everyone's adolescent fantasies included being famous and popular, and a bit of glamorous acclaim for the hard-working faculties at our nation's colleges and universities is never amiss. Furthermore, *U.S. News* performs a service by assembling and presenting data in a readable form, aimed at improving the public's understanding of higher education. The magazine can be congratulated for its acumen in moving to fill a marketing niche; the American public has a need and *U.S. News* is trying to meet that need, with profit to itself and to society.

Nevertheless, higher education is uneasy with these competitive rankings. Our critics suggest it is because we have something to hide. Yet our professional organizations conduct numerous surveys and data exchanges that are hardly top secret, though I grant they are not readily available at the local newsstand. Perhaps a truer and fairer criticism is to say that we are uncomfortable with popular surveys because we are among those who can't see the institutional forest for the trees. We know the separate value of each, its leaf and fruit, the kind of life it supports, how many can be sheltered under its boughs, and the contribution of each to the balance of nature. In other words, higher education is not so much a survival-of-the-fittest business component in a competitive, market-driven economy as it is an essential element in the ecology of a thriving democracy.

So here is the crux: despite the pleasure of seeing Duke University ranked number five among the "big schools" in the popular press, we can't help but wince when the university is referred to in the raw language of the marketplace as one of the "true educational conglomerates," a "brand name" with a high recognition factor among consumers. And when we are informed in the tones of overwhelming popular mandate that institutions of higher education are going to have to "operate more like the business enterprises they really are than the scholarly societies most would like to remain," we have to wonder, how would that benefit the society we were uniquely created to serve?[4]

There appears to be a fallacy abroad in the land that because higher education serves an economically competitive society, it should therefore duplicate the practices of that sector of society in every way. But rather like the invention of civilization, colleges and universities, in this country at least, were created to provide a place for the cessation of hostilities, where the tools of survival could be laid aside for a time, while the tools of the mind and spirit are sharpened. How, then, do we interpret the ethos of competition in this special environment?

I conceded earlier that higher education does operate by many of the laws of the competitive marketplace; our colleges and universities are, after all, designed to serve the society that created them. But clearly it is all too easy for the values of that marketplace to pervert the goals of healthy competition in the context of education. I think the American public understand this perfectly well and quite properly have been expressing their concerns about it. Let's consider two of the pertinent examples I cited earlier.

As a psychiatrist leading an NCAA school, I have become especially sensitized to the value of athletic competition as an educational tool for developing psychological resources in young people. The list of character traits I have in mind, however, any good parent or educator can name: traits such as self-discipline, self-confidence, a sense of fair play, and cooperativeness. Participation in school-sponsored sports is important in the development of leadership skills, offering practice in group motivation, conflict resolution, goal-directed behavior, personal initiative, and team bonding—skills that help create leaders for

4. Quotations in this paragraph are from, respectively, Jeffrey L. Sheler et al., "America's Best Colleges," *U.S. News & World Report*, Oct. 16, 1989, 66; Mel Elfin, executive editor of "America's Best Colleges," letter to H. Keith H. Brodie, M.D., May 2, 1990; and Sheler, 55.

every profession and every sector of our society. These are objectives clearly relevant to the educational mission, and intercollegiate athletic competition and athletic scholarships are meant to serve these goals. But when college sports are viewed as a profit-making enterprise and when athletic scholarships are regarded more as tools of the trade in a business venture than as educational opportunities, then we find ourselves faced with a perversion, a misuse of an otherwise beneficial form of competition.

A less blatant example, but one that is nonetheless drawing heavy fire these days, is the question of the extent to which competition for so-called "superstar" research professors may be perverting the teaching mission at our universities. This also is a legitimate concern; achieving a balance at top-ranked research institutions like Duke is a struggle at times because we are striving to assemble a faculty that is superb at not one but two extraordinarily difficult creative tasks. We are competing for the most brilliant minds, those that on the one hand can discover and create knowledge, while on the other can value highly and be stimulated by the process of sharing with the young. These are our requirements; they are almost, but not quite, impossibly demanding. To meet them, we must take care that two values, the value of knowledge and the value of transmitting that knowledge, are not made incompatible by an inappropriate competitive ethic.

Thus, in both the instances I am citing, in athletics and in academics, we must reinterpret the competitive ethos so that it serves education, pledging not to compete for the most brilliant and talented regardless of their personal goals and values. Whether we are seeking basketball players or professors, we want the very best of those who can benefit from or bring benefit to the educational enterprise. Not all talent belongs in the classroom, and not all competition need be conducted in the marketplace where the ethic is sell to the highest bidder and the consequences be damned.

Too much of the marketplace isn't good for education. In fact, it appears to be the case that too much of the marketplace isn't good for the marketplace either. Lately, even the gurus of the M.B.A. and the captains of industry have been worried about perversions of competition and have softened accordingly some of the maxims of the profit motive. More and more, they are sounding like college presidents and commencement speakers as they talk about serving the future and earning some of the fruits of the spirit.

For example, the controversial economist and dean of MIT's Sloan School of Management, Lester Thurow, ushered in 1990 by telling the *Atlantic Monthly* that America's business elite must "have a change of heart . . . to do the things that are good for [the country] in the long run, even though they may hurt a little bit in the short run."[5] Last month the chief executive of Glaxo Holdings told students at Duke's Fuqua School that "Running a business is not just about . . . keeping our country competitive. . . . It's about duty. It's about responsibility. . . . [It's about] stewardship."[6] And just two weeks ago the *Wall Street Journal* reported the findings of a prestigious panel of business school deans who called for changes that include screening M.B.A. candidates to measure their "concern for the consequences of [their] actions upon others," and curriculum changes that will counter "narrow, materialistic perspective[s] about business."[7] This hardly sounds like a groundswell of support for importing even more stringent marketplace credos into education. This sounds to me more like a call for importing the values and concerns of our educational institutions into the marketplace.

5. Charles C. Mann, "The Man with All the Answers," *Atlantic Monthly*, Jan. 1990, 62.

6. Ernest Mario, "World Needs Builders, Not Raiders," *News and Observer* (Raleigh, N.C.), May 27, 1990, 7J.

7. Gilbert Fuchsberg, "Business Schools Get Bad Grades," *Wall Street Journal*, June 6, 1990, B1.

What Americans mean by "competition" is a curious thing, both practical and romantic. We see it as a useful tool for building self-esteem, as an antidote to laziness, a spur to achievement; as a synonym for an economic system, a corollary that makes our political system work, and as a process that helps to create what our grandparents used to call "rugged individualism." But individualism is a romantic idea, too, that embraces both self-determination and the valuing of each individual human being. And this overriding concern for human life as an absolute value in and of itself, is what we believe to be the most important element, the "bottom line," if you will, for the conduct of a democracy.

And so we come full circle in our thinking, from open competition for a place at the table to a respect for human life that ultimately requires giving up our place to something else: to duty and self-sacrifice, responsibility to the community, and the obligations of the winners to help those who have fallen behind. Education is what enables us, as a society, to close this circle.

We best serve our nation when we protect the places where education goes forward. The best education proceeds in a fragile yet powerful environment where the competitive struggle is muted and the competitive ethic serves the time and place of joy and curiosity. At its level of highest achievement, education liberates and sparks the soul; even at its most basic levels, it opens up the world, frees the mind, and gives to each person the refined use of our most human tool, the brain.

Competition does not teach the love of learning. That is reserved to time and innate gifts and those who love to teach and learn themselves. As educators you and I are charged with the long slow growth of human beings and the consequences for a future we will not be around to see. Let us make the best use we can of the tools that come to hand; let us hold our special ground for the contests yet to come.

The Benchmarks of Community

In the preface to this volume we spoke of an overarching theme of the responsibilities of citizenship that permeates the speeches and my reflections on the Duke presidency. Citizenship, of course, presupposes a community of which one feels rightfully a part and to which one owes something in return. More than any other racial or ethnic group, African Americans have consistently found their rightful participation in predominantly white communities questioned, and academic communities have proven to be no exception. In fact, nothing in the late twentieth century has tested our American ideals of academic community and dutiful citizenship more than the troubling questions and besetting sins that swirl around the issue of race.

Looking back, I realize that the twin themes of community and race were constants—perhaps even definitives—throughout my presidency, and so it is not, after all, surprising that my last report to the faculty should be less an exercise in reminiscence and praise than fifteen minutes of painful recognition and admonishment. Undeniably, our focus on increasing the number of black professors at Duke had created tensions among the faculty, strains that showed in incidents of incivility and breakdowns in collegiality. Yet I would still say that whatever the strains, whatever the costs, it was and is the right thing to do. Today, as affirmative action comes under vigorous attack in the courts, in state legislatures, and in systems of higher education, the arguments advanced against it are familiar to me, having long been voiced by those opposed to affirmative action initiatives at Duke. To the argument that affirmative action legitimizes the dividing force of racial and ethnic differences, I would respond that there is something perverse about the idea of ignoring differences in a nation that was created by waves of immigrants who proudly brought their ethnic identities with them along with their desire to be part of a new nation. To those who say we should emphasize color blindness, common bonds, and equal opportunity for everybody, I ask how we can seriously claim that equal opportunity is available for everyone when we well know the poor quality of public education in many parts of our country. To those who say it is not the business of the university to redress the wrongs of history and remake society, I ask how we in higher education, in good conscience, can take a position of passivity when we well know that we hold the keys to the kingdom—admission to a better life, acknowledged membership in the community. For education is the means by which an inclusive society is built.

It is our responsibility to help; if we do not, the alternative is greater and greater polarization of racial and ethnic groups in our society and a larger and larger underclass. If the cost at Duke was a level of communal discomfort at times quite high, the investment was worth it. Far better to countenance that discomfort and draw attention to it than to cling to the idealization of a philosophy of "color blindness" and "merit" that had led to my being the seventh president of the university, yet the first ever to appoint a nonwhite vice president.[1]

ADDRESS TO THE DUKE UNIVERSITY FACULTY
JANUARY 21, 1993

For those who are counting—and I admit to being one of that group—today's address will be my eighth and final report to you

1. I appointed two black officers: Leonard C. Beckum, University Vice President and Vice Provost, and Janet Smith Dickerson, Vice President for Student Affairs, who was one of three women I named to vice presidencies, also a rare occurrence at Duke.

as president of Duke. In years past I have shared with you my assessment of the state of the university, reporting with facts and figures on the progress of our hopes and plans for building, financing, and peopling a university of increasing excellence and international breadth. And along with the nuts and bolts and the bottom lines, I have brought before you from time to time my reflections on how well we have lived up to our definition of ourselves as a community of scholars bound by shared ideas, values, and goals, that this definition might serve as a kind of philosophical benchmark against which all of our bottom lines must ultimately be measured.

Four years and nine months ago the Academic Council—the representative body of the Duke faculty—voted to establish a very specific benchmark for our definition of ourselves. As you will recall, that resolution of April 21, 1988, required that "each hiring unit within the university . . . increase the number of black faculty (at regular rank) over its present number . . . by at least one, before the fall of 1993. . . ." The resolution was accepted by the administration and approved by the Board of Trustees. It is my purpose today to review with you the specifics of this resolution point by point, to report on our achievements to date, and to describe and evaluate our efforts as a faculty in meeting the goals we have set for ourselves. I have chosen this focus because it is an important issue for me as president—the resolution is one that I supported—and because ultimately, our efforts, in concert with the efforts of colleagues at other research universities, will have important implications for the future of our nation.

To point one, then. Since September 1 of 1987 (the date specified in the resolution), 16 hiring units have succeeded in adding 19 black faculty members at regular rank. Those hiring units include the administration, 7 departments in the arts and sciences, the Divinity School, engineering, Fuqua, law, and four departments in the Medical School. Out of a universe of approximately 56 hiring units this is a discouragingly small number. Even more disappointing is the net increase in black faculty over the same time period: we began counting as of September 1987 when the university had 31 black faculty members at regular rank; currently we have 36 in 20 hiring units. This small net gain of 5 professors is accounted for by the loss, during the same period, of 14 faculty in 10 hiring units who left for varying reasons: resignations, retirements, or, in the case of 4 of these faculty, transfers to non-regular rank or administrative positions within the university.

Let me pause here to acknowledge that there has been some question about just what we mean by the term "hiring unit" in the context of the Black Faculty Resolution, and so I have asked the Deans' Council to develop a formal definition so that we can be consistent in our application of the term.

Returning to point one of the resolution, you will recall that all hiring units which have not fulfilled the requirement of increasing their black faculty at regular rank before the fall of 1993 must submit documentation of their recruitment efforts and propose a new recruitment plan (as outlined under section 3). I will ask that this information be provided by July 1, 1993, for review by our equal opportunity officer Vice President Leonard Beckum, by the provost, and by the appropriate deans. In addition, this information will be shared with the Committee on Black Faculty of the Academic Council.

Among the strategies utilized for increasing black faculty (as recommended under point two of the resolution) has been the visiting professor program. Although our database for visiting appointments is not as accurate or complete as for regular rank appointments, we know that since September of 1987 more than 19 black faculty have joined us as visiting professors, at least 4 of whom have stayed on at regular rank. It is important to note that many of these visiting appointments have been made in hiring units that have not yet been able to add a black faculty member at regular rank, such as anatomy, cell biology, civil engineering, international studies, mathematics, music, and zoology. While, as the resolution emphasizes, "A visiting black professor . . . does *not* meet the goal," such appointments are a clear signal of progress in identifying black scholars and building a network of those who may be willing to identify other promising black candidates. In addition, these visiting scholars increase our diversity, as do our other nonregular rank black faculty, surely a valuable interim goal. In these two categories, nonregular rank and visiting, we currently have 40 black faculty.

Section four of the resolution wisely addresses the future by focusing on our black graduate students. I am happy to say that we have more than doubled the number of black doctoral candidates enrolled since 1987, with a commensurate increase in funding. This was the goal we had set for ourselves. In the fall of 1987 we had 21 African American students studying for the Ph.D.; by this past fall that number had been increased to 52. In 1987–88 total funding for graduate students of color[2] was a little over half a million dollars [$540,636]; in 1991–92 we were able to provide more than $1.1 million [$1,179,845], as shown in figure 1. Breaking those figures down, you can see that the majority of this growth in annual support has been for African American doctoral candidates, from just under $300,000 [$293,201] to close to $800,000 [$786,730] in 1991–92, as shown in figure 2.

I must say here that the university has not yet complied with item c under section four, the instruction to "set up and fund fellowships for black graduates of Trinity College and the School of Engineering to study elsewhere . . . for four full years in pursuit of a Ph.D. degree." We have made it our priority to spend at Duke all the dollars we could raise for the support of our own black graduate students, and we will probably continue to funnel resources into the support of our own. We seem not to have developed a postdoctoral program as a way of increasing the pool of potential black faculty, as recommended in the Academic Council

2. Graduate students of color = Black, Hispanic, and Native American.

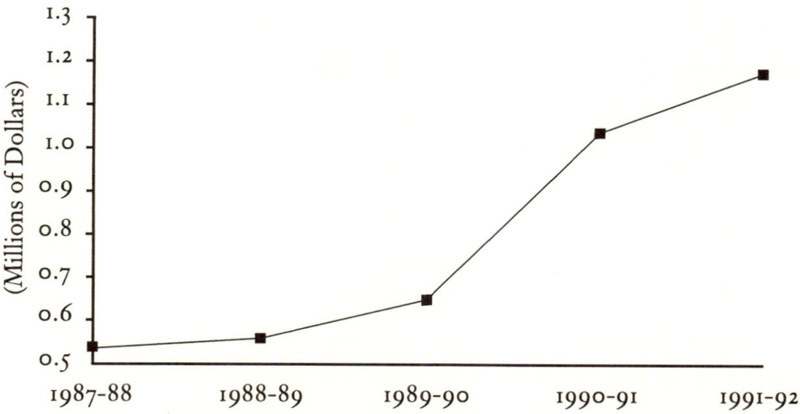

Figure 1. Duke University Graduate School Support for Students of Color

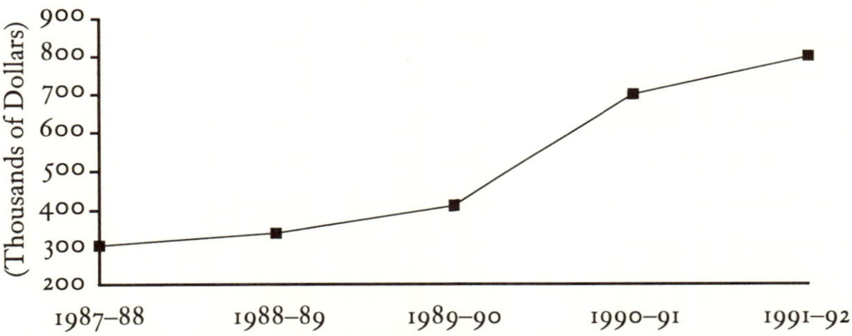

Figure 2. Duke University Graduate School Support for African American Students

resolution. Rather, we have encouraged and provided funds for departments and schools to make visiting appointments of promising black scholars, including those at the postdoctoral level, providing resources, I believe, to meet the spirit of this instruction while not limiting the use of those resources to the postdoctoral level alone.

The increase we have achieved both in numbers of black graduate students and in dollars has required the commitment of numerous faculty and members of the administration, of course, but

Table 1. Applications, Admissions, and Matriculations, 1987–92, for African American Students (Duke University Graduate School*)

	Fall 87	Fall 88	Fall 89	Fall 90	Fall 91	Fall 92
Applications	95	84	110	104	160	205
Offers of Admission	36	30	43	48	42	42
Matriculations	16	12	19	25	16	15
Full Enrollment	40	46	50	65	63	71

*Includes both masters and Ph.D. candidates.

I especially want to commend the successful efforts of our assistant dean for graduate school recruitment Jacqueline Looney, who joined us in 1987 specifically to begin intense targeting of students of color. A close look at applications, admissions, and matriculations of black students since that year shows a rise in applications from 95 to 205, while admissions and matriculations show a less dramatic increase, as demonstrated in table 1.

These numbers warn us not to be complacent about our success in increasing the population of black doctoral students. Certainly financial support is extremely important, but where stipends and living arrangements are more or less equal, faculty support becomes an issue. We know that the faculty's scholarly reputation attracts outstanding students. But these students' decisions to come to Duke and to remain and complete their Ph.D.s will inevitably be affected by the interest we show in their coming here and by the intellectual and psychological support we provide during their years of study. So far, the good news is that since 1987 we have succeeded in retaining 71 percent of our black Ph.D. candidates, a rate that augurs well when compared with Bill Bowen and Neil Rudenstine's recent figures showing a completion rate among all doctoral candidates of only about 50 percent.[3] Recog-

3. William G. Bowen and Neil L. Rudenstine, *In Pursuit of the Ph.D.* (Princeton, N.J.: Princeton University Press, 1992), p. 105. Bowen and Rudenstine note the

nizing the great need to increase the pool in many disciplines, we should give some credit to departments that, although not yet successful in adding black faculty either at regular or nonregular rank, are currently training doctoral candidates. These include biochemistry, cultural anthropology, pathology, pharmacology, psychology: social and health sciences, sociology, and statistics.

Let me now complete this summary review of administrative and faculty efforts to date in honoring the black faculty resolution so that we may turn to a few thoughts about the future. On the administrative side I assure you that every strategy recommended in the resolution has been attempted; that we have actively and regularly checked with all the deans, who have been responsive and hard working; and that verbal reviews of schools and departments have been conducted all along the way—in other words, we certainly have not waited for the Academic Council's deadline to expire before monitoring the progress in every area of the university. We have stayed in touch with our commitment.

Among the faculty I have seen much conscientious support for this undertaking—support that is not fairly represented by citing only the small number of hiring units that have been able to add tenured or tenure-track black faculty thus far. By combining all of our lists, we can gain at least some sense of the overall efforts at Duke to increase the African American presence on the faculty. According to our best count, 40 hiring units—better than two-thirds—have succeeded in contributing in some substantive way to those efforts and to our hopes for a more diverse, more representative, more fully and broadly American professoriate.

So, where do we go from here? How do we meet a goal that after nearly five years of strenuous effort still eludes us? I would like to offer three observations. First, there is no doubt that the lack of a well established African American studies program has

---

"sharp contrast" with completion rates in business, law, and medical schools of over 90 percent.

hampered our efforts to attract black scholars, both those who have an interest in working in this relatively young but vigorous field and those with different academic interests who view such a program as a rich source of colleagues and as a statement of commitment by the university. We are therefore determined to press forward with the search for a director of this program. Provost Langford is moving swiftly to build on the good work of our most recent search committee and expects to have interviewed two outstanding candidates before the month is out. A flourishing African American studies program is a key element in our minority faculty recruitment strategy and an important emerging area of research Duke cannot afford to neglect.

My second observation is this: no one seems surprised that, to date, the hard numbers of the black faculty initiative are disappointing, and there are those whose response is pessimism and a tendency to discount other results, such as those I have reviewed for you today. I will agree that, yes, we knew from the beginning that the resolution would present a challenge, but now is not the time to shake our heads over the difficulties and pronounce that we "knew all along it couldn't be done." Now is the time to wrest insight from hindsight—to review what we *have* done, to consolidate what we have learned, and to go forward with it. The resolution *has* made a difference at Duke. It has kept us focused. It has made the issue of racial supply and demand in the academic marketplace a constant topic, not just for discussion, but for measurable institutional action. It has sharpened our awareness both of the difficulties and of the needs. It has compelled us to do more than seek out today's talent and say we have done our part; it has forced us to take the long view and invest in tomorrow's black faculty with today's dollars.

Most of all, it has served to increase our individual personal responsibility, for the call to correct the underrepresentation of African Americans on the Duke faculty came, after all, from the Duke faculty, and it is the responsibility of each of us to contribute something positive to the efforts underway. And this brings me to—in fact is part of—my third and final observation on what further steps we might take to reach our goal.

Each member of the faculty at the very least contributes something to the climate of collegiality here at Duke. I spoke earlier of the importance to graduate students of finding supportive faculty to work with. Is it not equally important to faculty to find themselves among supportive colleagues? Do we not all prefer to do our work among people who value us, who appreciate our contributions, who invite our participation in the university? And would not a potential new faculty member prefer an environment where differing ideas and opinions are exchanged courteously, even encouraged by high standards of civilized discourse?

I would like to think that these are the prevailing conditions at Duke, but many of us can offer disheartening examples of departments where collegiality is at an unattractively low ebb—hardly appealing to gifted potential faculty. Most can recall the egregious instance, not so long ago, of a new colleague who received a public slap in the face via another faculty member's guest column in the *Chronicle*, where he was described as a "young black fiction critic . . . *prematurely*" [italics added] awarded a chaired professorship, among other less than welcoming comments. More recently, our reputation for collegiality could be said to be called into question by the *Faculty Newsletter*, which in the last issue chose to reproduce an attack in one of the British tabloids on our colleague Professor Stanley Fish, including reprinting a photograph of Professor Fish which the *Daily Mail* had labeled "Persecutor." This level of personal attack is, to say the least, unbecoming and serves no useful intellectual purpose. A review of the past year gives one the sense that the newsletter harps on certain issues such as so-called political correctness, women's studies, minority hiring, and racial issues in American society, in a tone best described by another faculty member on the publication's own letters page as "monotonous mean-spiritedness."

Such examples of community discourse among Duke scholars do nothing to convince new colleagues to join us—most especially those who would find themselves very much in the racial minority. Many of us forget at times, I suspect, just how much power we share and how far it can reach—power that can operate through negativity and passivity as effectively as through more positive and active efforts.

Let us remember that nothing affects the quality and character of the university so directly as the quality and character of the faculty. And because we do, after all, choose each other, we share primary responsibility for who we are, who we become, and therefore what the university will become. Earlier I spoke of our philosophical benchmarks. In surveying, a benchmark is a point of "known or assumed elevation from which other elevations may be established." The black faculty resolution stands as one of the means by which we hope to raise ourselves to higher levels as a faculty. It sets a worthy goal we must labor to achieve. As such it will continue to serve us well as a challenging benchmark of character and a statement of our values as a community of scholars.

Index

H. Keith H. Brodie, M.D., is President Emeritus and James B. Duke Professor of Psychiatry and Behavioral Sciences at Duke University. Leslie Banner, Ph.D., served as Special Assistant for University Affairs during the Brodie presidency.

Library of Congress Cataloging-in-Publication Data
Brodie, H. Keith H. (Harlow Keith Hammond), 1939–
Keeping an open door : passages in a university presidency / Keith Brodie and Leslie Banner.
Includes index.
ISBN 0-8223-1862-8 (alk. paper)
1. Duke University—History—20th century.
2. Brodie, H. Keith H. (Harlow Keith Hammond), 1939– . 3. Duke University—Presidents.
I. Banner, Leslie. II. Title.
LD1732.D82B76 1996
378.756'563—dc20 96-8678 CIP